HAUNTINGS

HAUNTINGS

Dispelling the Ghosts
Who Run Our Lives

JAMES HOLLIS, PHD

CHIRON PUBLICATIONS

ASHEVILLE, NORTH CAROLINA

www.ChironPublications.com

Re-released in 2015 under ISBN 978-1-63051-349-8 for distribution purposes.

Book and cover design by Marianne Jankowski.

Cover art: *Spectral Presences*, by Jill Hollis, oil on canvas.

"My Ghost" from *Everything Else in the World* by Stephen Dunn, © 2006 by Stephen Dunn. Used by permission of W. W. Norton & Co. Inc.

Paul Hoover, "Theory of Margins," used with the kind permission of Paul Hoover.

Gunnar Ekelof, "Etudes III," translation by Robert Bly. Reprinted with the kind permission of Robert Bly.

Printed in the United States of America.

Library of Congress Cataloging-in-Publication Data
Hollis, James, 1940-
  Hauntings : dispelling the ghosts who run our lives / James Hollis, PhD.

     pages cm
  Includes bibliographical references.
  ISBN 978-1-888602-62-3 (alk. paper)
  1. Autobiographical memory. 2. Subconsciousness. 3. Influence (Psychology) 4. Ghosts--Psychological aspects. I. Title.
  BF378.A87H65 2013
  155.9'2--dc23

                                                        2013014253

This book is for

Jill

Taryn, Jonah, Seah,

and

Timothy, who is always with me

———

With special thanks to Liz Harrison,

agent and friend,

and

Siobhan Drummond,

whose fine eye was most helpful in the manuscript

. . . the ghosts who let you sleep,
who speak, if they speak at all,
into the ear closest to the pillow,

offer you assurances of dawn
while their vaguely palpable bodies
touch you like a strange wind . . .

—STEPHEN DUNN, "SLEEPING WITH GHOSTS"

CONTENTS

Spectral Presences

This is not a book about ghosts in the usual sense of that term. There will be no Ebenezer Scrooge on these pages, no ghost of Marley dragging his lockboxes behind him to mess up the day for a miserly narcissist. But we all drag such noisy metallic boxes behind us. Can you not hear them? Can you not see them in your family? Can you not see them rippling through the pages of the daily newspaper? Henrik Ibsen did, and well before depth psychology as we know it came to be. He deeply intuited the impact of unexamined history upon the present. After all he called his 1882 play *Ghosts*, for he felt that his Oslo contemporaries were governed by invisible presences: dead ancestral influences, dead values, and deadly scripts to enact. And thus he has one of his characters say,

> But I'm inclined to think that we're all ghosts . . . it's not only the things that we've inherited from our fathers and mothers that live on in us, but all sorts of old dead ideas and old dead beliefs, and things of that sort. They're not actually alive in us, but they're rooted there all the same, and we can't rid ourselves of them. I've only to pick up a newspaper, and when I read it I seem to see ghosts gliding between the lines. I should think there must be ghosts all over the country—as countless as grains of sand. And we are, all of us, so pitifully afraid of the light.[1]

James Joyce—who spent his brilliant, wretched, fugitive life in exile, writing only about his accursed/beloved Eire—came to a similar conclusion in his 1914 story, "The Dead." He knew that he had to leave his country, his church, and his family. What he loved most, because it was governed by the past—foreign hegemony, the oppressive church, the burden of tradition, collective expectation, and practice—no longer truly loved him, valued him as the unique soul he was. So, when he looked around the bustle of Dublin he saw not life but death, and the gradual graying of souls by the weight of that collective burden. Thus, "One by one they were all becoming shades. Better pass boldly into that other world, in the full glory of some passion, than fade and wither dismally with age."² And thus he flung himself into a life of poverty and exile, supported only by his much put upon Nora and his own, obsessive, mythopoetic genius.

Contemporaneously, his countryman W. B. Yeats obsessively chased ghosts, joining several societies who sought direct connection with the spirit world, among them the Hermetic Order of the Golden Dawn. His wife, whom he first met in one of these societies, allegedly channeled the voices of this spirit world, who came, fortunately, to "bring him metaphors for poetry."³ Several of his twenty-six plays, including his last, the 1938 *Purgatory*, dealt directly with the presence of the other world in the affairs of this one. During the same era—a time between the erosion of biblical literalism and the demonstrably inadequate surrogates of contemporary culture—Carl Jung discovered that his mother was a medium; he attended more than one séance and later wrote his medical school doctoral dissertation on the "voices" which came through one of those occult encounters as embodied in his equally mediumistic cousin Hélène Preiswerk. But he too was not satisfied by their answers; he searched for and, I believe, found a psychological explanation for those disembodied voices and, having ruled out fraud and chicanery, explored ways those spectral presences might be honored without being literalized.

In Jung's heuristic studies, and his mapping of the rich terrain of the human psyche, we move from fear, superstition, and projection triggered by encountering the profound mysteries of the world we inhabit to understanding that all mental events, finally, are *within* us. No matter what we encounter in the outer world, whatever its autonomous, material form, we experience it, process it, and value it through our individual and collective psychologies. So it is, and so it has been, although there are those who have been burned at the stake for saying so.

The task before us, then, is to consider more fully how we are all governed by the presence of these invisible forms which move through us, and through history, and to understand them psychologically without "psychologizing" them. To psychologize is to reduce something to a merely mental state. Throughout most of recorded human history people have believed in ghosts and the like: daimons who visit both poets and the mad, angels who reportedly mediate the spiritual orders, not to mention incubi and succubi, and a host of other psychic phenomena and states of possession. Our predecessors considered the contiguous boundaries between visible and invisible worlds highly fluid, highly permeable. Jung has described this pervasive phenomenon:

> Among primitives . . . the imago, the psychic reverberation of the sense perception, is so strong and so seriously coloured that when it is reproduced as a spontaneous memory-image it sometimes even has the quality of an hallucination. Thus when the memory image of his dead mother suddenly reappears to a primitive, it is as if it were her ghost that he sees and hears. We only "think" of the dead, but the primitive actually perceives them because of the extraordinary seriousness of his mental images. This explains the primitive's belief in ghosts and spirits; they are what we simply call "thoughts." When the primitive "thinks," he literally has visions, whose reality is so great that he constantly mistakes the psychic for the real.[4]

There are mysteries, to be sure, and we will never fully understand the ineffable dimensions of our lives. Yet to understand them "psychologically" is to obtain two gifts:

- greater possible personal freedom through understanding from whence come the influences which govern our daily lives, and how we might bring consciousness to oppose them when necessary and serve them when desirable;
- and to understand that so much of what bewitches the ego into literalism and slavish service can be seen in depth for what it is—a received, inherited, culturally contrived energy system and not one rising from "the gods" or from our soul's holistic intent.

But to begin this study, I have to confess that this particular book began with a "haunting" of sorts, a disturbing presence that would not go away until I began to pay attention. I was finally obliged to ask, Why have you come? And what do you want of me? These are disturbing questions, but to flee them produces only compensatory symptoms and further haunting.

∾ ∾

One morning I awoke with an intriguing dream whose motifs were peculiar, puzzling, even hilarious, but nonetheless imperious. I dreamt I was in my house with my wife and daughter (both the house and locus were amorphous, anonymous). I had been instructed by someone that in the other room was the body of General Grant, yes, that one, Ulysses S. Grant, leader of the Union Army and later eighteenth president of the United States. It was my ambiguous charge to guard or protect his body until some anonymous authority would arrive to pick it up and deal with it properly. In the strange logic of dream life, I did not question this assignment, but took it on without question.

From time to time I would walk into the other room and look at the form, which was covered by a blanket. After a couple of such visits I noticed the blanket had shifted, progressively revealing a bit of the body. I asked my companion if she had moved the blanket, but she demurred. I visited the room again, and the blanket was further disturbed and now revealed the upper torso of the late general. Knowing this was peculiar, I looked around for other "agents" who might have moved the blanket, even air currents that might have ruffled the covering, but saw none. A subsequent visit revealed that the body itself had shifted position and now had a grimace on the countenance, one that suggested annoyance.

With considerable apprehension, I bent down and whispered in the face of the general, "Are you angry." There was the mildest stir, and I heard a faint grunt from the corpse that sounded like "yes."

At this point I fled the room and told my companion, "He is alive, somehow . . . alive!" She suggested that I call some authority and tell them that the general was still alive. So, for some reason not clear to me, I called a pharmacy instead and told them, "General Grant is still alive, and oh, by the way, I need some pens!" To my dismay, the pharmacist who answered cut me off and shifted me to the pens department, and I felt intense frustration that the real message—the general was still alive—had neither been delivered nor grasped. At that moment, the alarm clock rang, and I was summoned to a day of work. I felt deep dissatisfaction that I would not know how that dream would come out. It felt, as dreams often do, as if it had taken place over several hours rather than minutes. Moreover, I preferred to know the ending to the story rather than respond to the responsibilities of that day, and I suspected that the ordinary world of appearances and obligations would once again trump an aperture into the extraordinary other world of dreams.

As I stood in the morning shower I puzzled over the dream, smiling at its bizarre imagery. Then a quote of which I am quite fond came to mind, and I understood why this dream had been presented to me by whatever intrapsychic powers exist. The observation is from the novelist William Faulkner, who once opined that "the past is not dead, it is not even past." I then understood the meaning of that dream in the context of my present life.

I am at a point in the aging process, and in my professional life, where I would like to throttle back a bit. I have burned the tires to the nub or, in the words of West Texas, been "rode hard and put up wet." I had already published my thirteenth book and decided that one was the last one! Surely by now I had said everything that I had to say—the last two chapters modestly addressed the riddle of death and asserted that the meaning of life is found in the journey and not the destination. What else is there beyond such themes? And frankly, I was tired of hearing myself talk. At the same time, now, as had happened with my previous books, there were occasional nudges from the unconscious: a flash of a picture, a half-formed thought, an intimation of some task coupled with a feeling response. For me writing is both a joy and a pain, as it is for most people. It is what I find most mysterious, most onerous, most imperious and demanding, and most rewarding in the doing, or better, the having done it . . . and I was thoroughly tired of it. As the novelist Thomas Mann once observed, "writing is an activity which is especially difficult for those who are writers," and I wanted a normal life for a change.

What could be wrong with coming home and talking more to my wife, or watching the Rockets game, or reading a book hammered from someone else's smithy?

Still, one theme keeps coming back to me in personal life, in daily psychotherapeutic practice, and in watching the spectacle of history unfold in its familiar ways: *the persistence of the past.* We all believe we are self-made people, living consciously, making right choices, meaning well, and only when the consequences pile up around us do we ever question this presumption. On those dolorous occasions we may even be driven to ask, What is really going on here? Who is in charge of my life, really? Collectively, we live in a culture that discards the past as irrelevant, and individually we are convinced that we create ourselves anew every day. But as a therapist in dialogue with a client, working in this palpable world every hour, hour after hour, it has been ineluctably forced upon me that we also swim in a tenebrous sea of "timeless" time. It is not that we are dwelling in the past in our therapeutic work, but we are inevitably impelled to witness that the present moment is informed by the past, driven by its imperatives, its prescriptions and proscriptions. Either we are repeating it by serving its message, or trying to escape it, or we have evolved our unconscious "treatment plan" for it. Either way, the past calls the shots, at least until it is flushed out into the full light of consciousness. But who really wants to deal with the possibility that they might be repeating or running from their parent's lives rather than living their own? Who wants to look at the possibility that we are dumping bad karma onto the generations that follow us?

I have also learned, by personal experience, professional training, and clinical example, that there is a deeper intelligence than our egos at work in the lives of all of us. (What, after all, produced this weird dream? I certainly did not conjure it forth from any conscious frame.) Our egos are fragile wafers on a vast sea, even as our separate biographies float in the flotsam and jetsam of histories not our own. Sensing its fragility in this overwhelming mare nostrum, the ego inflates its importance and proclaims, mostly to itself: *I know who I am; I am in charge here; I know what I know; and what I know is sufficient to make proper decisions for myself.* Sometimes, more often frequently, the aftermath of such inflation obliges reconsideration and recrimination, and we wonder, What was I thinking? or we recognize that there were other factors at work than those of which we were conscious at the moment. Such moments of insight are humbling, even humiliating, but from them we gain a grudging sense of the presence of the invisible in the midst of the visible world.

Now, back to the bizarre dream of the dead general who, it seemed, was *not* dead. I had recently read a new biography of Abraham Lincoln, given that we have celebrated his bicentennial anniversary, not to mention having grown up in Springfield, Illinois, and having Lincoln as an inescapable part of my psychic tapestry.[5] Grant, another citizen of Illinois, was not someone I was drawn to, although I must admit I was profoundly impressed by how he, like the great Rail-Splitter, had, through persistence, gone on to a large destiny after a series of first half of life failures. I also was moved by how, given his parlous presidency and the economic turmoil of his day, which parallels that of the present, Grant, dying of cancer, heroically wrote his autobiography to help support his family. (There were no talk shows then or affluent groups that would pay handsomely for a celebrity to visit and utter banalities, as recent politicians are doing as I write.) Rather, in the face of pain and despair, and imminent death, he summoned himself to write. He finished the book that would support his family just days before he died of cancer.

Could it be that this image might have some meaning to me? Could it be that the corpse was "angry" because he was being treated as dead when he wasn't dead yet? Could it be that, contrary to my will, I was entrusted with this responsibility for the past, that my lethargic consciousness around just "sitting with the dead" was no longer permissible, and that whether I wanted to or not, I was being directed by some authoritative other to the pens department? What, one wonders, would one be expected to do with a *pen*? Could it be that the autonomous psyche was calling me back to my vocation, quite independent of the ego's whining desire for surcease, and that, as Jung observed in his essay on the attainment of personhood, the summons to live our journey is a *vocatus*, a calling forth, quite separate from one's conscious desires? Could it be that the Self, the superordinate wisdom and purposive energy of each person, has little interest in my comfort or my petty wishes but has at least one more assignment to give?

To think so would, in the climate of our fugitive, hedonistic time, either be pretty peculiar . . . or pretty compelling.

For the reader who is new to the work with the psyche, the dream of General Grant seems like a bizarre fantasy, the kind we all have and dismiss as silly: the product of indigestion or a replay of what we saw on the late night news before going to sleep. I used to believe that. After all, what could be more improbable than the muse showing up, unbidden, in the form of General Grant? But I have spent the last few decades working with the invisible world that drives this visible plane and now know better. I knew enough to not dismiss the dream even though at first I thought it both humorous and opaque. I also know enough to keep worrying it about, and slowly, inevitably, through a long day of appointments with others, fragments of insight floated to the surface: the dead are not dead; the Illinois lads rebound and push through fatigue and imminent defeat until they arrive at destiny; destiny commands, whether with pen or sword, and imposes a sacred obligation to show up in the face of one's desire for a normal, casual life.

Such engagements with mystery are what life calls us to. *It is not what we want but what life, apparently, wants of us.* To believe this, one then has to believe also in mystery of some kind, that is, that we are more than merely material bodies that dance awhile and then just rot away. If we really understood this life, it would not be mystery, and whatever we understood would only be a petty artifact of the limited tools of conscious life. There are other forces afoot of which consciousness has only the dimmest of understandings, though our ancestors have reported similar encounters, and left behind quite disparate accounts, for millennia.

Do any of us really believe that we are here to make money and then die? Are we here just to propagate the species anew? Why bother then? Why not just "lose, and have done with losing," as Samuel Beckett wrote in *Endgame.* What animates this matter at birth, courses through us, registers its opinion through our autonomous feelings, our somatic and energy systems, and then departs at death? What drives our species to the symbolic life, whether it be a concerto or a concentration camp? What does life ask of us, and how are we to answer that summons? Does life matter, in the end, and if so, how, and in what fashion? As children we all asked, indeed lived, these questions, and many of us have forgotten them in the steady drumbeat and reiterative abuses of daily life. But our choices reflect our values and our putative answers to these questions, whether we are conscious of them or not. Being more conscious then is both a summons and an obligation. My dream was a summons, and this text is an obligation.

And so this is the beginning of my next book. It is not my choice, at least not the "I" who addresses the reader directly at this moment. It is, however, not "I" as ego consciousness, but some other "I" who is called into service, who timorously steps out onto the road, marching south toward places unknown, into the unconscious. Years before me those other Illinois sons marched to many strange, terrible, compelling places with magical names like Chickamauga, Shiloh, Manassas, Chickahominy, Spotsylvania, Antietam—opalescent jewels on a skein of suffering. They, too, surely, were weary and afraid, and still they went, and we honor them for going. Who knows what magical places we will be brought to visit in our time, for the forces that move us all course deeper than we can ever understand. The past is not dead; it is not even past. And what we resist will persist—as *haunting*.

Notes

1. Henrik Ibsen, *Ghosts and Other Plays* (New York: Penguin, 1964), 61.

2. James Joyce, "The Dead," in *Dubliners* (New York: Dover Publications, 1991), 152.

3. W. B. Yeats, Introduction to *A Vision* (New York: MacMillan, 1938), 8.

4. C. G. Jung, *Psychological Types*, vol. 6, *The Collected Works of C. G. Jung* (Princeton, NJ: Princeton University Press, 1971), par. 46.

5. Michael Burlingame, *The Inner World of Abraham Lincoln* (Champaign: University of Illinois Press, 1997).

CHAPTER 1

The Haunting of Untold Stories

There's always someone haunting someone—haunting someone
And you know who I am
Though I never leave my name or number
I'm locked inside of you . . .
— CARLY SIMON, "HAUNTING"

To ordinary consciousness, we seem to be corporeal bodies, mostly, fixed by gravity and stitched by pain and mortality to this gravid earth. But we are, rather, systems, energies, exchanges, projections, programs, force fields, and continuous enactments of tenebrous scripts both conscious and unconscious. What animates this assemblage of matter that we inhabit when we are born? What blows *spiritus* into the lungs of the bawling infant? That *spiritus—ésprit*, re-spiration, in-spiration—is energy, a force field blowing, blowing through eternity into time-bound bodies whose curving trajectory brings them inexorably back to earth. Even as plummet-bound bodies, decaying, dying as we lurch through life, we remain nonetheless force fields of energy, dancing on the grave of history and aflame with eternal fires.

When I think about "story," I think of a shaping spirit, an informing intentionality. We may call it narrative, plot line, and, cumulatively, biography, with a predictable end but with infinite permutations along the way. As Hemingway reminded us, if you don't have the hero die at the end, you just didn't finish the story. But is that the story, really, the only story? Perhaps. Perhaps not.

If we could materialize our invisible psychic life, make it tangibly visual, we would perhaps see it as a congeries of energy streams. We would acquire a much more psychological perspective if we could transform most of our nouns into verbs. It makes for inelegant English, for sure, but we need to think of the Self as an energy source "selving" and our stories "storying" through us. Our ego, in service to understanding and the need for control, converts the elemental processes in life into nouns. We foolishly convert even "the gods" into nouns, into objects "up there," looking down, rather than metaphors for the autonomous, mysterious energies of the universe. The ego reifies its understanding of being, oversimplifies it, concretizes it, and tries to fix it in service to stability, predictability, and, most of all, control—all in the face of the transforming, autonomous nature of "naturing." In every moment, the ego is driven to fixate, stop, grab hold of, and control, even while cells are dying, rebirthing, and transforming, even as psychological matrices enact their recondite agendas as well. Understandably, we are obsessively compelled to ask what provides unity amid this discontinuity. What offers an answer to Goethe's paradox, "*Was Dauert im Wechseln?*"—what provides continuity amid change? what abides amid transience?

The answer of the theologues is that God is the abiding presence. Or, as the Jesuit poet Gerard Manley Hopkins wrote in the nineteenth century, in a poem celebrating the abundance, variety, and multiplicity of this concrete world,

> All things counter, original, spare, strange;
> Whatever is fickle, freckled (who knows how?)
> With swift, slow; sweet, sour; adazzle, dim;
> He fathers-forth whose beauty is past change:
> Praise him.[1]

To the Buddhist, the idea of permanency is delusory. All is flow, transition, passing, especially this transient ego state. To the conventional ego, identity is memory, intention, as well as the manifold structures we create and which then define us. To the depth psychologist, it is the Self that, transcendent to the ego, provides autonomous continuity, even when memory fades or trauma intrudes. Thus we breathe without ordering the lungs to their inhalant labors, autonomously pounding primal tom-toms in the scarlet chambers of the heart, pushing oxygen through the capillaries to outlying provinces, and metabolizing sugars and proteins in service to the hearty appetites of blood, bone, and beef.

Who or what but a reality superordinate to the ego is running this bizarre operation? What but a transcendent, yet inner, presence could attend all these operations and get it (mostly) right? And what guiding intelligence weaves the threads of an individual biography; what hauntings of the invisible world invigorate, animate, and direct the multiple narratives of daily life? Timeless sagas unwind their narrative skeins in each of us: a *genetic* story, older than memory; an *archetypal* story that forms, shapes, and directs in service to adaptation and meaning; a *socially constructed* story, such as gender, or race, or class, by which we are so often bewitched as to grant them ontological status despite their fictive origins. And then there are the compelling complexes which are splinter stories, splinter identities, splinter scripts, splinter mythologems.

We all have complexes because we all have a history, and history charges our psychic life with energized clusters of valence. Some complexes exercise a benign, protective role in our lives. Without some positive experience of bonding and trust, we would be prevented from forming commitments and relationships. Yet others bind us to trauma, immaturity, and outdated prejudicial perspectives. The recrudescence of these fragmentary histories invariably usurps our purchase on the present and plunges us into our replicative pasts. Some complexes even dominate an entire life.

Consider, for example, the pathetic story of Franz Kafka. One of history's keenest writers, he lived miserably with his parents in Prague, loathed himself, sabotaged his relationships with women, and suffered numerous psychosomatic illnesses. What produced all this? His domineering father, miserable in his own life, convinced his son that he was similarly miserable and effectively doomed Franz's journey. Franz's only respite from this spiritually infested home was through an aesthetic sublimation of his suffering, producing luminous attempts at self-analysis through his strange parabolic stories and paradoxes. Even then he attempted literary suicide by requesting that his *oeuvre* be destroyed (a request fortunately refused by his friend and executor Max Brod). Twice he was engaged to Felice Bauer but backed off from marriage. Their concrete embodiment felt too incursive, and so he remained distanced, aloof, spectral. "Letter writing," he once observed to Fraulein Bauer, is "an intercourse with ghosts, not only with the ghost of the receiver, but with one's own, which emerges between the lines of the letter being written . . . . Written kisses never reach their destination, but are drunken en route by these ghosts."[2] Apparently, forbidding spectral presences stood between these two and intercepted those kisses. One is reminded of E. E. Cummings's remark in "since feeling is first" that whomever pays attention to the syntax of things will never wholly kiss you.

A friend of Kafka observed that Kafka served a god in which he did not believe. Do not we all so serve such residual, resident "deities"? Do not we all serve spectral presences, primal complexes, ghostly admonitions, ephemera which bind us to our past? Do not we all worship at the shrine of the dead every day, and does not such unconscious bondage reduce the scope of the life we might otherwise be living?

What would you do if you were free, unfettered by the claims of the past? Just today I spoke with a client who had reacted with tears and sleeplessness when she had to reverse herself and seemingly break her word to another. It was not so much that the demands of the situation required her to change course, but that such a posture placed her back in the realm of childhood where the ill opinion of another was not only scary, but potentially lethal. No wonder she could not sleep. Another client, a therapist in supervision, lamented her rage against her dying parent, how it floods her with guilt and ambivalence, and how it creeps into her work with her own clients. When one has resided long enough in a toxic zone, one carries the toxin within, always, and all one can do is flush it out into the realm of consciousness and wrestle with it. In the case of the therapist, she is summoned to an awareness that her attendance upon her mother may be compassionate but no longer compromised by the infant's need for her approval. Given that such approval never came, or at least was never freely found without crippling conditions attached, grants this spectral presence an immense power in her present psychic economy. She, too, continues to worship a god in whom she also no longer believes.

As for Kafka, most of his destructive turmoil derived from the untold story of his father and the perversity of a parent's personal problem. What unlived life, what self-loathing in the father served as a transferred spectral presence in the child's life to devour his son's spirit? How one wishes one could have intervened to help the child flee this psychic miasma and lead a normal life. But was Franz Kafka ever to have a normal life, born as he was into a haunted house, a house dominated by a father who doubtless had his own determinative ghosts harrying him into persecuting his own child, the simulacrum of his own lost, disconnected past? This is why Jung observed that the greatest burden the child must bear is the unlived life of the parent. That is, wherever the parent is stuck, the child will be similarly stuck and will spend his or her life seeking to overthrow such noxious stuckness, evolving an unconscious treatment plan whose purpose is to assuage the pain of the psychic burden of this static past.[3]

So, what is the "real" story of our lives? Are they all real or all unreal, all provisional? There are the stories we tell ourselves, and the stories we tell others. Some of them may even be true. But what are the stories which are storying their way through our daily lives and of which we are mostly if not wholly unaware? What are the stories that represent our rationalizations, our defenses, the stories in which we remain stuck like flies in molasses?

All of us suffer the fallacy of overgeneralization, namely, what was "true," or appeared true, remains a defining point of reference, a prompting script for us in ever-new situations. What past wounds to our self-esteem show up today in our deflections from our deepest truths or our overcompensation and grandiosity in reaction to scripts foreign to our souls? What stories did we acquire as children, what marching orders did we receive to serve in the remaining chapters of our history? Were we to be the unseen child, the fixer, the scapegoat, the marginalized? How do those stories persist in the present?

We know from depth psychology that we have coping devices which click in automatically and protect us, sometimes by denying stories, sometimes by identifying with them. Sometimes we project fractal scripts, palimpsests of possibility, onto others and then relate to them as if this is who they are rather than recognizing them as fictive characters in our inner drama. Thus we unwittingly seek out persons to play and replay our persecutors, or rescuers, or victims. Sometimes we repress stories, and their presence may only be surmised when they leak into our dreams, our bodies, our children, our anaesthetizing addictions. Sometimes we dissociate from or condemn others when they enact our secret lives and embody our shadow, which is always repulsive to the ego. The vastness of the human psyche is such that we will never know it fully, or even in significant measure. So we who pride ourselves on being conscious, lead lives in service to stories, some conscious but construed and witnessed aslant, some unconscious but persistent, and almost always binding us to a past over which we had no control. Given the ubiquity of these silent formative narratives, what is our alternative to struggling for a precious purchase on consciousness over against whatever agencies are there dictating our lives?

Let us look at two stories that remained untold and yet whose influences seeped into the reality of everyday life. The first story is the family narrative of my good friend Stephen Dunn, Pulitzer Prize–winning poet, and the second is the fictive account of novelist Bernard Schlink in his novel *The Reader*.

Stephen has written about this story in various poems and has given me permission to use it here, so I am not revealing something profoundly private, though it certainly was kept private in his childhood. Stephen told me once that he knew there was a frosty distance between his mother and father, but he didn't know why. His father would sit in his rocking chair at night and read and drink, and in the morning Stephen would find him with a half-empty bottle and half-finished book.

Stephen wrote of how he would be sent to fetch his father at the local pub and bring him home for supper. He worshipped his father, who once took him to see a hurricane whip up the frothing sea at the Rockaways, after which they were both scolded by his mother out of her protective, and equally correct, love. So the child sat between them, amid more familiar stormy weather, knowing that other, more opaque currents of destruction whipped about each evening repast. Given the child's limited purview, intuiting something was amiss, but lacking the powers of adult comprehension, what else was he to conclude but, "I must have thought damage / is just what happens"?[4] The child normalizes the abnormal. While his psyche "knows," and registers its seismographic readings, the child is unable to draw upon any powers to effect clarity, change, or resolution in the outer world.

What was that damage, one wonders? Why this estrangement? What were the causes? All remained lost until later, much later. Then, as Stephen wrote me in an e-mail, "I learned the truth of the situation from my father when I was sixteen. He was drunk, but what he said was clearly true, and he swore me to secrecy." Stephen learned that his mother had looked to their savings and found them missing. When she queried her husband, he lied to covered up a situation.

> The money went to my maternal grandfather whose mistress had been hospitalized. My grandfather had run out of money paying her bills, and he asked my father for help. He was never able to pay him back, and one day my mother saw the bankbook devoid of their savings and asked where it had gone. My father said he had lost it at the track, evidently not wanting to tell his wife that her father had a mistress. Grandfather died shortly thereafter; no one fessed up, and my father was treated as a kind of wastrel for the rest of his life. He died at fifty-nine of a heart attack. After an earlier heart attack, he had been told to stop drinking, but instead redoubled his effort.

So, a noble gesture, an untold story, becomes a spectral presence which haunts the family, ruins a marriage, and scars the life of the child. As Stephen further wrote me, "I loved all the actors. I know that the knowledge of these stories contributed to my silence, and to a lifelong proclivity toward ambivalence, of siding with every side." Notice those qualities of personality: silence and ambivalence. Perhaps useful in many life circumstances, but are they really chosen, or rather obliged? They remind one of Joyce's autobiographical character Stephen Dedalus, who said that he felt obliged to effect "silence, exile, and cunning" in order to protect himself and to pick his way through the thicket of his life.

Stephen Dunn's life and verse remain haunted by these perplexities. Two decades after writing of his parent's marital secret, he returns to the primal scene in a poem titled "My Ghost," in which he writes,

> An outgoing man, my father once held back
> a truth that would have rescued him from sadness.
> Now he roams the night, my inheritance
> In every word I hear him speak. He vanishes,
> returns, no place for him in this entire world.[5]

A truth that would rescue us from sadness . . . surely we ought to speak it now and free ourselves from such Sisyphean sorrow! But honor calls, truth is withheld, and silence and exile eventuate. Stephen's inheritance manifests every day in invisible but compelling ways. What place is there, then, for us in this haunted world?

Stephen's father died while his son was studying in Spain. That night Stephen and his wife were awakened by a pounding on the roof. There was no storm, no branch above, no natural explanation. In the morning a telegram from New York arrived saying that his father had died that very hour. Stephen and his wife were convinced, rational souls as they were, that it was his ghost pounding on the roof to be let in, or at least to say good-bye. It made no sense, but they were both terrified and both were summoned to the numinous mystery of haunting. Who is to say that that man's spirit was not in fact seeking a home, for a moment at least, or a farewell to what mattered in his life, in his passage from this spinning earth, the only home we know? And who is to say that, as Stephen intuits, his spirit does not still roam, an ancient mariner with the albatross of an untold story about his neck, seeking someone to hear and to welcome him home? Who is to say that in many of our moments there is not some unbidden spirit who seeks solace and welcome from us, as Philemon and Baucis respectfully welcomed the godly strangers who passed their humble abode? It is only when we welcome such spirits and give them entrance that they may reveal themselves to us. When we open to ask what comes to us, why it has come, we may grow and be enlarged by the dialogue that emerges. When we deny them entrance, they do not go away. They go underground, persist, perseverate, and prevail. All ghosts will tell us, if we listen, that we ourselves will come some day to say, along with Stanley Kunitz in "Passing Through," "I only / borrowed this dust."[6] When the dust is returned to this earth, the energy that animated it perhaps persists in other forms. At least it does not hurt to ask what that past might be asking of us. Then damage is not "just what happens," but rather is the residue that keeps on keeping on.

Only dialogue with such "stuff" provides release. The question of how we do this is addressed later in this book, but it suffices now to ask ourselves this very practical question: What do these powers, these issues, make me do, or what do they keep me from doing? Often, intuitively, we know the answer immediately, and if we do not, we keep asking the question until it comes to us at three in the morning, or in the shower, or while we are driving in heavy traffic. We do know, though often we do not know that we know.

࿇ ࿇

Another form of the untold story appears in the fine novel *The Reader* by Bernhard Schlink. A young man is taken in by an older woman who helps him, seduces him, and quickly captures his soul as only first love can. The youth obsesses about her, follows her at her job as a tram driver, and is frequently critically rebuked by her, all the while enjoying hot sex. Even so, she professes feelings for him and asks him to read novels to her. He introduces her to the classics that he is reading in school. She is as much hooked by the intellectual world these books open to her as he is to the sensual world she has opened for him. Mysteriously, she moves away, and he mourns her with the typical ghastly grief of the adolescent, the *Liebeswahn* or "love madness," which all of us have suffered at some time.

The youth goes on to graduate from the university and attends law school, where his international law professor takes the class to one of the war crimes trials which are then transpiring in post–World War II Germany. To his astonishment and horror, his seducer is sitting in the dock as one of several concentration camp guards accused of atrocities. Of all of the accused, she alone takes responsibility for signing a document that acknowledges their role in burning prisoners to death, and the other defendants are happy to let her. While all of the defendants are convicted, she receives the longest sentence.

The young man cum lawyer reviews her strange acquiescence to the charges being piled on and compares it with other memories of their time together. He realizes that the secret of her "untold story" is that she is illiterate, and she is haunted by this secret which is somehow more shameful to her than having been a guard at a concentration camp. That is why she asked him to read all those novels to her during their trysts. That is why she was working as a tram driver, because it was a job which did not require reading. That is why she confessed to the implicating document at her trial, because that monstrosity was still preferable to her confessing her shameful illiteracy.[7]

Jung observed that everyone has a pathological secret, something so scary, so shameful perhaps, so humiliating, that one will protect it at nearly any cost. As long as such secrets remain buried, they will continue to percolate their invisible toxins into the world of conscious life. As a therapist I have born witness to the confession of many such stories, which is both privilege and burden. Yet the telling of such, in the presence of a witness, often occasions a lifting of that burden for the client.

While the woman in *The Reader* is serving her years in prison, the lawyer goes through his own doomed marriage, doomed in part because nothing can compare to the intensity of that first love. But he also continues to read novels to the woman; he tapes them and sends the cassettes to her in prison. Through the long years, his fidelity to her is unshaken, yet for him the untold story that always sits between them is not her illiteracy but the nature of her work at the camps. Still he continues to send the tapes, and one day she figures out that she can begin to match his voice with the words in front of her in books borrowed from the library; painfully, diligently, she learns to read, an achievement she keeps to herself.

The day before she is released he visits her in prison—he is now middle-aged and she is elderly—and he makes it clear that while he will continue to help her, they will not be living together. Though he never specifies why, the implication is that the untold story of her role in the camps lies between them like a ghost, forbidding further intimacy. That night, her last night in jail, she hangs herself, leaving only a note stating that the money she has slowly saved is to go to a Jewish charity that teaches reading. Clearly this is her last will, and it testifies to the horror of her history.

When the lawyer finds out that she has learned to read, he also discovers that much of what she later came to read, studiously, was the history of the Third Reich, especially the history of the camps.

> I went over to the bookshelf. Primo Levi, Elie Wiesel, Tadeusz Borowski, Jean Améry—the literature of the victims, next to the autobiography of Rudolf Hess, Hannah Arendt's report on Eichmann in Jerusalem, and scholarly literature on the camps . . . . [The warden adds,] "As soon as Frau Schmitz learned to read, she began to read about the concentration camps."[8]

While her motive for suicide is not fully disclosed, it is certainly plausible that when she learned the untold story of her participation, her collusion in the greatest organized crime in Western history, she could not bear the thought of leaving her legitimate sentence behind for a putative freedom. The incredible paradox of this story is that by giving her the gift of literacy, the freedom of understanding a story larger than the immediacy of her environment, her lover also gave her access to the information that condemned her.

So, the untold story of her illiteracy, the untold story of their illicit affair, the untold story of her criminal history, the untold story of her part in history's nightmare, the untold story of our collective failures—all collude to haunt the present, infiltrate lives, and destroy them. *The Reader* additionally sheds light on the untold story of the millions who perished, their lives unlived, their stories cut short by thugs and by quite ordinary people who proved capable of murder, haunts all of Western civilization, for when our good people, our sacred and venerated institutions, and our humanistic traditions were put to the test, we failed. That story cannot ever rest untold.[9]

The narrator of *The Reader* explains that he finally had to write the story of their lives, their passionate engagement with each other, and their unexpected intersection with the dark plumb lines of history. While he seeks understanding, forgiveness, release from the haunting, he also knows,

> The tectonic layers of our lives rest so tightly one on top of the other that we always come up against earlier events in later ones, not as matter that has been fully formed and pushed aside, but absolutely present and alive. I understand this. Nevertheless, I find it hard to bear. Maybe I did write our story to be free of it, even if I never can be.[10]

ॐ ॐ

Tracking our ancestral origins is another means by which the untold story haunts and, like a drop of ink in a liter of crystalline water, slowly threads its way through and in time colors the whole. The earliest fictive fragments often ripple through the generations, forming barriers, deflections, admonitions, and play out their way until someone, through suffering or sudden revelation, apprehends their presence and breaks the chain. Such stories are our personal "foundation documents," whether we know them or not.

In James Agee's autobiographical *A Death in the Family*, he recalls summer nights as a child in Knoxville when the family left the dining room to sit on the porch, watch the bell spray of the lawn sprinkler, hear the susurrus of the cicadas, until fatigue captures the child's frame and he tumbles toward sleep. The people in the big bodies take him up to bed, lovingly, but did not then, did not ever, tell him who he was. Similarly, the young James Joyce, through his imagined persona, Stephen Dedalus, sits in school daydreaming and writes his name at the center of concentric circles, going out from his family, his school, his country, his Éire, his planet, to the universe itself in seeking to learn his real name and learn his real story. Both of them spent their adult lives assembling those stories and bring them into greater and greater consciousness.

Did we not all have these thoughts, these questions as children? Did we not all wonder whose story we might have entered? As a child, I wondered if the sky above me, which to my corporeal eye formed a great dome, was not a single dot in the brain of some cosmic dreamer, in whose dream I moved and seemed free but which could be ended at any second by the dreamer awakening or simply having another dream or thought. I was not a weird kid; I was simply thoughtful, and I intuited that there must be some such story, as yet untold to me, but which perhaps the adults knew well. (I remain somewhat disappointed to this day that I never found an adult with a story that makes any more sense than my childhood vision).[II]

What story, told or untold, threads its way through our DNA, our genetic coding, and plays out a same old, same old? Jung said that we could all be wiped out but for two, and the world would be reconstructed very much the way it is now, for after reproduction the genetically driven stories, the archetypal shaping energies that lie in all of us, would recreate patterns, dynamics, personae, and denouements in an old, old story, which forever renews itself. Anyone who does not know that today's headline is simply a passing variation on an old, old story is simply not very well educated in the human narrative. The same passages, the same stupidities, the same delusions, the same inflations and deflations, and the same returns to earth play themselves out over and over. The past is not past. The present is haunted by the archetypal dynamics which remind us that any story untold is an unconscious present. An unconscious present is a story which will insist on being told and will spill into our biographies. Over the entrance to his home, Jung carved a phrase from Erasmus: "Bidden or unbidden, God will be there." So, told or untold, the archaic stories ineluctably manifest through our unconscious choices, our aversions, our preoccupations, our projections, and our agendas and replay themselves in the recognizable patterns which constitute the human story.

How many of those who are insecure seek power over others as a compensation for inadequacy and wind up bringing consequences down upon their heads and those around them? How many hide out in their lives, resist the summons to show up, or live fugitive lives, jealous, projecting onto others, and then wonder why nothing ever really feels quite right? How many proffer compliance with the other, buying peace at the price of soul, and wind up with neither? We all have been here before, metaphorically, and we will repeat these scripts in ever new variety, wearing new costumes and brandishing new amulets, but they are the same stories. And we are never more haunted than when we forget this fact, that our lives are the variations upon central themes, the dialectical embodiment of which is both our fate and our destiny.

When Yeats considered the hysteria that seized his contemporaries in the late 1930s, he reminded them that, while ostensibly new actors stepped forth center stage, old dramas and old personages were once again enacting their scripted roles.

> All perform their tragic play,
> There struts Hamlet, there is Lear,
> That's Ophelia, that Cordelia;
>   . . .
> Though Hamlet rambles and Lear rages,
> And all the drop-scenes drop at once
> Upon a hundred thousand stages,
> It cannot grow by an inch or an ounce.[12]

All of us enact our inner Hamlet: though we know what we need to do, for reasons we do not know, we cannot do it, and thus we fret and dither about until our hand is forced. All of us are captive to our inner Lear, that insecure, narcissistic part that takes over from time to time and plays the lion to conceal the bleating lamb. Like Ophelia, all of us pine for what is not possible and end by destroying what is. And all of us yearn beyond measure, beyond intrinsic capacity, and are alternatively saved, condemned, and owned by that same yearning.

Gaelic, the ancient language of the Celts, which is still spoken in parts of West Ireland and Northern Scotland, has no word for the present. The nearest equivalent is a word that translates as "the continuing past." And so it is for us all. As a therapist, I see how each of us buys into a fragmentary narrative of some kind, a provisional story which we were told by others perhaps or which was imprinted on us by the fortuities of our time, place, and roles, or more commonly were our phenomenological "readings" of events and experiences. Naturally, we identify with these early fragmentary stories, serve their narrative scripts, and drive inexorably toward their dreary denouements. That these are received, not inherent, stories is something we have to learn the hard way, even though our symptoms, our addictions, our compensatory dreams are protesting our service to them from childhood to the present.

Whoever has given tongue, brought these internalized narratives to consciousness, attains a fragile purchase on this moment and, with that, new possible choices. Whoever can imagine, bring to consciousness, such figures as haunt our lives has truly become "psychological," that is, he or she is thus able to lend tangible image to the otherwise invisible currents of the soul. With such images we can become somewhat more conscious if we work at it, but we will not, over time, avoid playing out our drama just as it was written within a long time ago. Accordingly, we continue serving, running from, or trying to fix these narrative scripts, and we err to think that having once recognized them, they will quietly retire from the scene. Their staying power, any older person knows, is immense, and they resist our efforts to repress them or finesse them or distract them. But that does not keep us from trying to dispel them from our psychic attics.

Notes

1. G. M. Hopkins, "Pied Beauty," in Richard Ellmann and Robert O'Clair, editors, *Modern Poems: An Introduction to Poetry* (New York: W. W. Norton, 1976), 23.

2. Franz Kafka, *Letters to Milena*, trans. Philip Boehm (New York: Schocken Books, 1990).

3. It is beyond the purview of this book to consider the role of genetics as a different form of haunting, but one might ask, for example: Were the replicative, self-destructive immolations of the Eugene O'Neill family chosen, learned, or genetically driven? Were the suicides in the Hemingway clan, or the suicide of Nicholas Hughes, son of Sylvia Plath, choices or predispositions, or both?

4. Stephen Dunn, "Regardless," in *Landscape at the End of the Century* (New York: W. W. Norton, 1992), 33–34.

5. Stephen Dunn, "My Ghost," *Everything Else in the World* (New York: W. W. Norton, 2006), 24.

6. Stanley Kunitz, "Passing Through." Accessed at http://www.poetry-foundation.org/poem/179287.

7. In *Swamplands of the Soul* I tell the story of one inhabitant of such a concentration camp who had to make terrible decisions, not unlike the

situation in the novel *Sophie's Choice*, and, haunted as she was by this choice, she felt condemned to roam the earth and tell her story, struggling in vain to be released from her bondage.

8. Bernhard Schlink, *The Reader* (New York: Vintage Books, 1998), 205.

9. I address this capacity within each of us for the full range of motives and behaviors, however angelic or despicable, in *Why Good People Do Bad Things*. What lies unconscious, untold in our stories, tumbles into the world by the acts we perform, whether conscious or not. The shadow which trails behind each of us is the untold story that soon, perforce, becomes the collectively untold story of the world.

10. Schlink, *The Reader*, 217–18.

11. In his memoir, Jung recalls sitting on a rock as a child, thinking about the rock, and wondering whether the rock rather was thinking him. *Memories, Dreams, Reflections*, ed. Aniela Jaffé (New York: Pantheon Books, 1961), 20.

12. W. B. Yeats, "Lapis Lazuli," *Selected Poems and Four Plays* (New York: Scribner, 1996), 179.

CHAPTER 2

On Synchronicity and Quantum Physics

Science is uncommon sense.
—J. ROBERT OPPENHEIMER

I am writing this page on a Saturday in August 2009. In a few days I fly to Tampa, Florida, to address a conference devoted to exploring mind/body relationships. As I am often stuck in airports or waiting in a hotel, I always make sure I have something to read. As I reflected on what to take, it suddenly came to me that it was time to reread the *Meditations* of Marcus Aurelius. Thin as it is, it would fit easily into my carry-on bag. I had read the book some years ago, but why it came back to mind was wholly unknown to me.

I was checking my e-mail before going up to the attic to fetch the *Meditations* when I received one from a friend whom I had not seen or heard from in many years. In this e-mail he expressed his appreciation for the meditations of one Marcus Aurelius, which I had introduced him to many years ago but had forgotten. How could there be such an amazing confluence of thoughts occurring in two sensibilities separated by time and thousands of miles?

The following Monday I read in *The Writer's Almanac*, which I gratefully receive every day in an e-mail from NPR, that it was the birthday of a well-known poet. I always paid attention to this poet because he married a former college student of mine, Hilary, from New Jersey. One hour later I got an e-mail from a former client to tell me her close friend, the same Hilary, sent me greetings and thanks for a chapter I had written on death in my last book. It was helping her cope with the death of her husband, that same poet. I had not known that my former client and Hilary were friends, but the more important fact was not that NPR was behind the news of his death, but that there could be such a strange congruence of events once again.

That same Monday, I was thinking about ordering a book written by a friend of mine in Australia. When I got home that night, he had mailed me his book, unbeknownst to me, without our having discussed it and after a hiatus of communication of several months. The following Wednesday, I took advantage of a free hour to phone my brother who lives less than a mile from Wrigley Field in Chicago. He talked about going to a Cubs game and how close he was to the stadium. When I hung up I realized that my last client, a baseball fan, while an Atlanta Braves fan, had left his other cap on the chair, which read (of course), "Wrigley Field / Home of the Chicago Cubs." On Thursday night, while I was writing the paragraph in chapter 1 about wondering as a child whether we were part of some cosmic dreamer's dream, I recalled that there was a mythic reference to that same idea that I should look up. I closed the manuscript and went online to check my e-mail before retiring. In one of the messages, a colleague from Dallas referred to Vishnu's dream, in which we are all characters in the reverie of a cosmic dreamer. There is no way he could have known I was trying to remember that source.

I ask of the reader only that you accept my word that all of the five examples above—Marcus Aurelius, the death of the poet, the mailed book, the Wrigley Field cap, the allusion to Vishnu's dream—really happened as I have described them here. I have no motive to deceive in these matters. In fact, I am as befuddled as the next person at these remarkable, convergent events. I am sure you can likely supply analogous examples from your life, and I could also draw from the many I have heard from patients. Frankly, my rational side, which dominated the first half of my life, is still confounded by these offenses to our Western notions of causality. I understand the theory behind these acausal events, but a substantial part of my mind refuses to accept them. Still, they happened. Any one of these "coincidences" can be explained away as having some cause we have overlooked or as being within some sort of mathematical possibility, if not probability; however, I do not think so many occurring in the space of a few days can be explained in any other way than what Jung called *synchronicity*.

What is synchronicity, and can we explain such events? What

are their implications? Are they not also some form of haunting, the spectral presence of some kind of purposive energy infiltrating the apparent objective solidity of daily life? If there are such energies, how are we to explain them? Are we meant to explain them? And how are we to reframe our understanding of ourselves in this palpable world if such confounding mysteries exist?

Historically, the Western world prevailed in physics and chemistry, both of which explore the external, tangible, quantifiable world. Thanks to Newton and others, we gained enormous control over the forces of nature. I am grateful for this mastery every time I fly in a plane or drive a car or turn to my physician for treatment. Similarly, our sense of time and space are external, measurable, ostensibly predictable. One exists at a specific location at a specific time. Furthermore, one has a name, a defined locus, and a social role. These forms of measurement are arbitrary, to be sure, but they give you a point of reference from which you can obtain a sense of orientation. Whenever these "fixities" are shaken, the person, the tribe, the culture grow disoriented and suffer crisis. Because the alleged fixities of social order, race, gender, sexual orientation, religion, hierarchy of values, and so on, have been deconstructed over the past two centuries, shown to be social, not physical, constructs, less fixed than *nomos*, there is a high degree of cultural anxiety which takes the form of hysteria, shabby reasoning, and regressive, even violent, affect, and which seeks to repress such ambiguity by oppressing others.[1] This is the thinking of dictators, and the chronically insecure.

On the other hand, Eastern cultures have traditionally sought access to the interior world. Just as Western physics studies the external world, so such historic schemata as the *I Ching*, the *Tao Te Ching*, and many other healing or divinatory modalities address the inner life. The *I Ching*, to choose one example, utilizes a method that most Westerners would consider arbitrary or accidental to gain purchase on an interior causality. To the Western sensibility, casting coins or yarrow sticks seems fatally stricken with accident or chance, but the Eastern view is that the practitioner, in a meditative mood, enters the Tao of the moment, that is, participates in the *qualitative* dimension of reality. Thus the arrangement or conjunction of moments is not arbitrary after all but takes on the qualitative textures of time and space.

To choose a simple example: if two cars collide at an intersection, the Western mind asks who failed to yield, who violated the *nomos*, that is, the legal constructs we have evolved to guide the flow of traffic. The Eastern mind might rather ask what does it mean that we have met in this way. What does this "accident" ask that I become more mindful of? We could put it another way: *How does this accident oblige me to become more psychological?*

Like these forms of investigation, modern psychology has similarly split. On the one hand are the therapeutic modalities which identify behaviors and seek their correction, or recognize flawed cognitions and seek their reprogramming, or uncover biological imbalances and seek their adjustment. All of these efforts make sense and are useful. At the same time, any one of us would feel insulted if we were considered to be only the sum of our behaviors, thoughts, and body. Each of us would say something like, "But that is not who I really am; that is not my essence. I am more, much more than that." Another branch of modern psychology, the psychodynamic, understands that we all are meaning-seeking, meaning-creating creatures and that when we experience the loss of meaning, we suffer. Such suffering does not lend itself to quantification, and the forms of modern psychology addressing only that which can be quantified have suffered a failure of nerve before the larger question of meaning. Modern depth psychology asks questions of meaning and understands that the chief project of psychology is to solicit the meaning, the mystery, of the psyche in all its intents, especially in its pathology, its symbolic expressions. When we remember that the Greek word *psyche* means "soul," we have then entered the interiority of our lives. Too much of modern psychology, and almost all of the pop psychology one finds on talk shows and bookshelves, has forgotten psyche. The requirement that we restore psyche to psychology obliges us to enter the inner life in order to better understand and order the outer life.

Synchronicity is a manifestation of energies moving through the invisible world and entering the visible world as seeming coincidence. Does coincidence exist apart from synchronicity? I think it does, and coincidental events certainly lie within mathematic probability.[2] But there are events that manifest something other than mathematical possibility, events which call for an engagement with mystery and an enlargement of consciousness. These events ask that we consider whether there are other values to be considered, other perspectives to be honored, other framings to be invited than those that fall within the blinders of conventional, constrictive consciousness.

When, for example, one consults the *I Ching*, as I do infrequently precisely because I respect it so much, one does not ask how to further manipulate one's life from a conscious standpoint, but rather one submits a question like: "Of what should I be mindful when considering this career path?" "What different perspective is asked of me in considering the events which have befallen me?" Just today I spoke with a woman who was seeking a way to help emancipate her son as he approached the age of majority, which was complicated by the recent death of his father. When her son came home and told her he was moving out, and moving on, she was devastated. Yet his own psyche had told him exactly what was needed for him, for both of them, at that moment. What seemed traumatic and rejecting was reframed as the psyche's answer to the perennial dilemma of dependency versus separation needs.

Or consider this far more improbable example. A former colleague of mine served as a Texas Ranger during the 1940s. On one occasion his life was saved by another Ranger while patrolling the Rio Grande. Their lives took different paths when the two men entered different branches of the service during World War II. When he returned, long separated from his friend, and not in direct contact, my colleague undertook further education through the G. I. Bill and became a college professor in New Hampshire. One day, while discussing stories of rescue with his class, the professor began to tell his own story of rescue by his fellow Ranger. In the midst of the telling, the man walked into the classroom, having tracked down his old buddy twenty years after the event. How can one possibly explain this away as mere coincidence? For my colleague, who a sensate, "facts are facts" kind of guy, the incident helped compensate his psychic life by bringing a bit of mystery into it. Afterward, his sensibility enlarged, and he was even more aware of the presence of invisible energies amid his tangible world.

How can one go wrong in humbly asking the question, "Of what should I be mindful here . . .?" *Synchronicity* is merely a word that asks us to consider that there are, as Hamlet reminds us, more things in heaven and earth than we had heretofore considered. When I consulted the *I Ching* thirty-five years ago about whether or not to travel to Zürich to undertake analysis, and later, analytic training, the hexagram that came to me involved crossing the wide water and consulting the wise man. An image like this can be interpreted in many ways. Certainly at the ego-conscious level the wide water seemed like the Atlantic Ocean and the wise man seemed to be Jung. But at the intrapsychic level, it also meant to me to enter the vasty deep of the unconscious and to find the source of wisdom, the wise figure which dwells within each of us. That both of these images underlined, perhaps ratified, the decision to go to Switzerland was a reminder to take even more seriously the choice before me and take more seriously the short life we have to live. Affairs had become, in playwright Christopher Fry's words, "soul-sized" and demanded of me a soul-sized response. It was not that I had to consult an outside authority, which is what we learn to do in childhood; it was rather that I had to learn to consult the authority within, wherein I recognized what I wished, needed, had to do. The *I Ching* was telling me what I already knew.

So what could the synchronicities I described at the beginning of the chapter mean to me? There is no definitive answer. As we approach mystery, consider how to explain it, we inevitably are reminded that if we can explain it casually or causally, it is not mystery. So, I am left to ponder these convergences of events piling on top of each other in the middle of a heavy work schedule. I conclude that their meaning for me, which is the only meaning I can possibly grasp, is that they were calling me back to something. What, perchance? I think they were reminding me, during a series of days when I was preoccupied with outer demands, that the inner world also makes demands, and when we forget this, the consequences begin to pile up. Additionally, I had stopped writing this book for awhile—distracted, yes, busy, yes, but also lazy in that I did not fight fatigue and torpor and distraction and "show up." Most of life involves our showing up, and we have so many ways of not showing up. Our popular culture is a vast array of protections, distractions, and soporifics, lest we be obliged to show up.

Since I mentioned Marcus Aurelius, what would he have to say about my spiritual, intellectual desuetude? He wrote this reflection, not in the sybaritic retreat of a Roman mansion, but on the Danube frontier, cold, wet, and fighting the barbarians who threatened his life, his nation, and all he held dear.

At day's first light have in readiness, against disinclination to leave your bed, the thought that "I am rising for the work of man." Must I grumble at setting out do what I was born for, and for the sake of which I have been brought into the world? Is this the purpose of my creation, to lie here under the blankets and keep myself warm? "Ah, but it is a great deal more pleasant!" Was it for pleasure, then, that you were born, and not for work, not for effort?[3]

Well, now, it is rather hard to contend with Caesar Marcus Aurelius on this front, is it not? How could I not show up, despite the outer and inner obstacles? These synchronicities did in fact pull me back to my task, the task of approaching mystery again, of engaging the hauntings of daily life by the ineluctable forces of the invisible.

What then does this have to do with quantum physics, and why should we care? The other speaker at the conference in Florida, Dr. Amit Goswami, is a quantum physicist, and part of my job was both to learn from him and to dialogue with him on the subject of the healer and the healer's relationship to the mystery of healing.

While Newtonian physics still works for us, keeping airplanes in the sky mostly and bridges from collapsing without reason, we have known for a century now of phenomena that do not behave according to the expectations of ordinary observation, of electrons passing from one orbital path to another without traversing the distance between, of particles that appear in two places at once. We have become obliged, in short, to undermine the fixities of materialism with more sophisticated questions and more sophisticated observing instruments. Ever since Danish physicist Neils Bohr (1885–1962) asked his questions and made his observations, the causal loci of time and space aptly described by Newtonian physics no longer seem to apply. Simply by observing phenomena, we change them, concluded Werner Heisenberg (1901–1971), given that we both participate in a common force field. Chaos theory shows us that even apparent randomness, or chaos, serves patterning processes from a source transcendent to ordinary consciousness, ordinary causality.[4]

Just as a trompe l'oeil obliges us to reframe our conscious standpoint in order to view the object from more than one angle, so quantum physics obliges us to understand that the fixity of the object is only a sensation from one illusory perspective, while from another it is entirely different. So the new physics reminds us that what we take for the fixity of the object is but our momentary observation of energy systems, systems that are forever transforming themselves every millisecond. From whence this phenomenon originates is a mystery, a mystery some have called God in the past. (Consider the ancient saying, found in many sources, that "God is a sphere whose circumference is nowhere and whose center is everywhere.") This nonlocal insight of the mystical and intuitive tradition is now being confirmed and ratified by the new physics. Thus, some "consciousness" transcendent to ordinary human consciousness not only "makes" matter but drives the patterns of its transformative manifestations as well.[5]

The new physics confirms the insight of Jung that an archetypal energy field organizes chaotic energy into patterns of meaning, and thus we all move to cosmic rhythms. What Rupert Sheldrake called "morphic resonance" is analogous to what the ancients intuited as "the music of the spheres." Just as nature organizes and drives in service to the fulfillment of the potential of the object, so psyche organizes the chaos of energy into developmental systems in which individual objects are portions of a universal drama. In his memoir, *Memories, Dreams, Reflections*, Jung observed that we may achieve all of the objects our ego desires and still feel disconnected and adrift unless we also intuit ourselves part of a cosmic drama through which we also experience nonlocalized connectivity. So my fantasy of what we might call Vishnu's dream was not off the mark after all. Robert Oppenheimer, who penned the epigraph at the beginning of this chapter, also understood the archetypal resonance of the moment when he observed the first nuclear blast at Alamogordo, New Mexico, and quoted Vishnu, "Now I am become Death, the destroyer of worlds."

So what is this about, really? Recall that I was flooded by these synchronicities in which we find an oxymoronic acausal principle at work. While I was attending to my outer work demands quite faithfully and, I would like to hope, effectively, these synchronistic images piled up on me to push me to remember the inner work as well. Recall the e-mail from a former student that launched this series of events, and his quote from Marcus Aurelius reflected on how all the pieces of our sundry worlds may fall harmoniously into structural unities. What I was forgetting was that the disparate parts of our busy world, which so easily can fall into disunity and neurosis, are also in service to profound currents that seek to shape and move us toward greater personal consciousness, on the one hand, and, on the other, the progressive surrender to participation in a cosmic consciousness. To put it bluntly and concretely, having the groaning, grunting General Grant appear in my dream life was not enough to get me moving in a sustained way. So, whatever energies first produced that dream regrouped, revisited me, and got me mobilized anew, to both my dismay and aroused motivation.

Standing before the awesome majesty and magnitude of the universe is so intimidating that many of us cry out for mediators—the state, gurus, evangelists with coifed hair—all with their own agendas of gain. The purveyors of the marketplace frequently denounce those who learn to respect their own encounter with mystery as "gnostics." Well, *gnosis* means "knowledge." If I can learn from my direct encounter with mystery, if I can feel myself moved by the energies of the universe, and am haunted by them when I ignore them, then why not live my life according to *what I have learned directly*, rather than what is mediated by others, however sincere their motivation may be?

Some distrust such splintered revelation, even consider it the route to madness, and flee encounters with the invisible energies that in fact course through us on a continuous basis. Is it not a paradox that the chief practical function of so many religious organizations is to protect people from religious experience? Are they afraid that the faithful might go off the reservation? Still, as William Wordsworth observed of his imaginatively driven contemporary William Blake, many considered him mad but he plumbed depths not known to the sanity of others.

When we can acknowledge the presence of the invisible in our visible worlds, as my dream and those intrusive synchronicities recalled for me, we truly appreciate the symbolic life and participate once again in the mystery of which our individual journey is such a tiny but inestimable part. The flight from these mysteries, the flight from the summons to look within, shows up over and over as symptoms, somatic disorders, or troubling dreams. In his 1900 *The Interpretation of Dreams*, Freud cited as his epigraph, "If I cannot persuade the higher powers, at least I can stir up the lower." Stirred as they are, the lower powers enter the quotidian world as haunting.

This book exists because of the movement of invisible energies. My conscious intentions were not enough; in fact, they sabotaged the necessary work of writing. So it would seem the invisible powers—call them gods, demons, muses, or whatever metaphor one prefers—took over and began to nudge, then push in their various annoying ways. I believe that each of us experiences such nudging from the unconscious world all the time, but we have learned to suppress and repress these entreaties in service to a more comfortable status quo ante.

The truth is unsettling: if we are to recognize the powers of the invisible world, however understood, then we have to broaden and deepen our view of our lives, continuously reassess our values, and make more difficult choices. We have to embrace a psychology that goes deeper than behavior modification and cognitive reprogramming. If we open to this possibility of an invisible, dynamically active world, we then live in mystery anew, a prospect both inviting and daunting to the power-driven, comfort-seeking agendas of a dilatory consciousness. As Jung observed, "The least of things with a meaning is always worth more in life than the greatest things without it."[6] This book exists not because I wanted it to, but because those telluric powers refused to stop their irritating haunting. As the twelve-step programs aver, "what we resist will persist."

We may add to that: what we resist in time becomes pathology, either through platitudinous, superficial lives or embodied as addictions, depressions, or obsessions with those objects upon which the unlived life has been projected. We may confess instead that what we resist will persist, as haunting.

Notes

1. Millennia ago, the Greeks recognized *nomos* as how socially ordered experience becomes normative for much of our lives.

2. By the way, the creator of the mathematic construct we call probability theory, which underlies so much of our ability to anticipate the range of the possible rushing toward us, was both a mystic and a mathematician: Blaise Pascal.

3. Marcus Aurelius, *Meditations*, trans. Maxwell Staniforth (New York: Penguin Books, 1964), 77.

4. Between Einstein's four papers in 1905 and the Solvay conference in Copenhagen in 1927, the essential stability of the Newtonian world was overthrown and even the most sophisticated physicists plunged into mystery after mystery. While that mystery persists, many current technological innovations have derived from a theoretic model still evolving, still far from finished.

5. As I write, physicists at CERN in Switzerland are announcing the confirmation of what is hyperbolically called "the God particle," or Higgs boson, which seems to be an elemental catalytic in the formation of matter.

6. C. G. Jung, "The Aims of Psychotherapy" (1931), in *The Practice of Psychotherapy*, vol. 16, *The Collected Works of C. G. Jung* (Princeton, NJ: Princeton University Press, 1954), par. 96.

CHAPTER 3

The Ghosts of Our Parents

When the wind blows wrong, I can hear it today.
Then my mother's worry stops all play

And, as if in its rightful place,
My father's frown divides my face.
                              —NAOMI REPLANSKY, "AN INHERITANCE"

Our biographies, our psychic lives, our impulses toward the world are historically contained and yet driven by forces that transcend consciousness and individual intent. Consider, for example, that we are apparently the only species that, being mortal, is also conscious of our precarious purchase on this world. Life brings us two gifts: a moment in time, and the consciousness of its brevity. We owe life two things in return: a life fully lived, and the gift surrendered at the end. But consider also that how we view this journey is profoundly influenced by the lens through which we see the world.

When I was a child, just after World War II, I received a pilot's fur-lined helmet and goggles as a gift. Naturally, I wore this gear as I flew at a fairly low altitude, perhaps four feet, to school each day. What was remarkable about the goggles was that one could insert different colors of Plexiglas in order to adapt better to climatic conditions. I waited eagerly for a foggy day so that I might see the world through a yellow lens. The green lens produced a green world, and quite different features emerged from the world as presented through the other lenses. Even as a child I could not help but be aware that I was seeing the familiar world in an unfamiliar way simply by changing the lens. Later, when I learned that our eyes have lenses as well, this variegated reality continued

28

to bubble up in disturbing questions : What *is* the world, I wondered, and how is it that I see it so variously, depending on which lens I use?

Unwittingly, naively, I had backed my way into philosopher Immanuel Kant (1724–1804), who used the same metaphor of blue spectacles to indicate that we never know the *Ding an sich*, that is, the thing in itself, but only our subjective experience of it. Our subjective experience is, of course, our reality, strained as it may be through our physiology and our affective and emotional screens. Do we ever, as separate physiologies, separate psychological lenses, separate planets, see the same orange, the same apple, at the same moment? Hardly. We have our personal, subjective experiences of them, and our highly eccentric experiences interact with that presumptive external reality and alter it profoundly. (While we need experience to ground reason, lest we fall into seductive delusions, we also need reason to critique the traps of subjectivity and its tendency toward overgeneralizing.) Unwittingly, I had also backed into Werner Heisenberg's (1901–1976) principle of indeterminacy, which asserts that our experience of the world is a highly interactive, dialectically changing engagement of "world" and "experience of world" in which each is altered by the other. In short, we are ineluctably driven to the necessity of psychology, namely, the recognition that all we experience is flushed through our subjective apparatus. Moreover, psychology is tasked with the troubling paradox that its chief summons is to bring clarity to how we experience the world, and how we distort it in the very moment of experiencing it. We are obliged to wonder, can we ever really understand something from an objective remove when we are also swimming in it?

Similarly, we need to employ a phenomenological perspective, which asks that we not speculate on the nature of ultimate reality, which we cannot know anyway, but rather observe *how* we are experiencing it. As Edmund Husserl (1859–1938) and a host of other phenomenologists insisted, we are obliged to study the *experience* of the world without presuming we know or understand the world. But we can observe and bear witness to subjective experience through such categories as perception, emotion, or even meaning or its absence. Each of us operates within a received *Lebenwelt*, or frame of cultural experience, which has ground the lens, and construes the world anew, as well. Such a "life world" is a framing lens, both aperture and limitation at the same time. Do I experience the same blueness of the sky as you do? At what moment? Do I experience the same reality as you do when one talks of happiness? Do you and I have a common experience of the idea of God?

How can we possibly relate to each other when we live in such idiocentric isolation from one another? Fortunately, we have invented useful contrivances—images, signs, languages—which have a common, albeit fictive, representational ground. The language of mathematics is more or less common throughout the world as a fictive representation of proportion, duration, process, and relationship. A red octagon shape on a roadside now represents "stop" in almost every country. As we move up the ladder of abstraction, however, we are obliged to employ metaphor and symbol to point toward the ineffable rather than name it. What do we mean when we say *love*, or *justice*, or *beauty*? Certainly we have conventional definitions of these experiences, but our experience of them, and what we mean when we utter these words, varies immensely. And what do we mean by *nature*, or *god*, or *meaning*? If they were merely nouns, pointing to objects, could we then find them in South Dakota, or Bolivia, or Samarkand? Is not our essential condition, then, that of members of a species that desperately seeks to stand in relationship to presumptive reality, and to other members of the species, while swimming all the while in uncertainty?

Even worse, as Ludwig Wittgenstein (1889–1951) reminded us, we fall into bewitchment by our own contrived language games and think we are speaking of reality when we convert verbs into nouns like *nature* or *God* or *meaning*. He suggested that if we really understood how we grow enchanted and imprisoned by the very tools we have evolved to help us navigate the world, then we would need to just shut up for awhile. ("Whereof one cannot speak, thereof one should remain silent," Wittgenstein concluded in the final sentence of his *Tractatus Logico-Philosophicus*.) But we babble on nonetheless and periodically try to kill our neighbors in defense of our bewitched condition. How many armies have marched off to slaughter their neighbor in the name of their *God*, the *true* God, unaware that they have actually violated boundaries shouting, "Our metaphor is better than your metaphor"? (As Joseph Campbell once observed, *myth* is other people's religion.) Understanding that the metaphor only points toward mystery, but is *not* that mystery, would seldom if ever inflame the hearts of youth to go off on a jolly venture to kill their neighbor.

So what does this have to do with parents? Everything! No influences in our lives, no grinding of the lens by culture, no newly learned experience plays as large a role as that played by parents in the formative life of the individual. We receive our genetic inheritance from them and with that not only our somatic tendencies, aging patterns, propensity to certain disorders, and lifestyle predilections, but the actual physiological apparatus of our perceiving and processing tools: eyes, ears, brain, et al. But as obvious as this physical inheritance is, and as pervasive an influence, a *Lebenwelt* in itself, the psychological influence is even greater. Fundamental percepts of how we see the world and ourselves in it are derived from the internalization of these primal presences, or primal absences, in our lives.

As tiny, vulnerable beings, we are largely at the mercy of the conditions our environment presents to us—economic, social, cultural—which define roles, scripts, ways of seeing, ways of not seeing, values, and so on. The *Lebenwelt* of a medieval, agrarian Buddhist living in Thailand a thousand years ago will have a quite different lens through which to see and value the world than a young businessperson in Montreal in the twenty-first century. But even more, we internalize the specific messages, our subjective renderings of messages, and their implicate and explicate models of behaviors which we observe around us as essential teaching devices for the engagement of self and world. Is the world safe? Will it meet us halfway, or more? Is it trustworthy? Is it invasive or abandoning? And if so, how are we to cope with that? Inevitably, each child internalizes a Weltanschauung of self and world and a set of reflexive adaptive stratagems whose purpose is to manage anxieties and to get one's needs met as well as possible in a limited universe.

If one experiences the world repeatedly overflowing one's boundaries, for example, the core message internalized is that the world is powerful, and we are not. This core percept of generalized powerlessness leads to systemic adaptive patterns of avoidance, a compulsive power drive to get control of that environment, or reflexive compliance, or multiple combinations of the three. Each strategy is an embodied interpretation of self and world, reflexive in character, and a protective adaptation that in time gains such a purchase on one's life as to become one's operant way of being in the world. In other words, our internalized interpretations drive our daily management systems and create patterns with which we become acculturated and come in time to call our lives.

In the face of the uncertain other, the abandoning other, one has a tendency to internalize the discrepancy between one's needs and the limitations of the other and form various provisional, essentially unconscious hypotheses. Among these hypotheses may be, for example, doubts about one's worth, having internalized the limitations of the other as a statement about one's own intrinsic suitability for nurturance. From such diminished self-worth arise both patterns of avoidance or self-sabotage and patterns of overcompensating grandiosity. Or one may suffer narcissistic wounds, which are treated by the manipulation or control of others to more adequately reflect and feed one's unmet needs. Or one may be driven by an inordinate need for reassurance and connection, which births addictions and dependencies of all kinds. In the momentary "connection" with the other, the existential horror of disconnect, abandonment, is assuaged, but only for a moment, and therefore the compelling drive to repetition is reinforced, institutionalized within.

Each behavioral pattern is replicated so often as to become a locked-in mode of being in this contingent world. Each pattern is a derivative, fortuitous vision of self and world, driven mostly by the internalization of the parental engagement, an interaction that is ubiquitous, overwhelming, exclusive, and most often "the only game in town." So who would contend, then, that the primary haunting of adult life is not the internalization of those parental presences that drive, deflect, repeat, and necessarily distort our voyage through this essentially unknowable universe?

Predictably, we will see only what our lenses allow us to see, lenses ground and refined by the millions of repetitions of early life. Naomi Replansky's lines at the beginning of this chapter are a confession that, for all the miles she may have traveled in her emotional life, the parental models she lived with were internal-

ized as apprehensions, and impose themselves upon her, no matter how vigilant her consciousness.

Here is a another example of this primary haunting: Celine's
mother recently died after a long illness. She dreams, "I am in
my childhood home, taking a shower alone. I emerge from the
shower and feel someone is there in the house. I am scared. I
open the front door and cross the threshold and that is scary too."
We have more questions here than answers. Why has the dreamer returned to the childhood home? Is that her mother's presence
lingering in the house? She never sees anyone in the house. Why
does opening the door and walking outside, crossing a threshold,
also seem frightening?

While we cannot definitively know the answer to these ellipti-
cal questions, nor even fully why we dream, nature never seems
to waste energy, so dreams are surely part of the self-regulation of
our natural system. Jung believed that dreams both process and
metabolize the immense onslaught of daily life and compensate
for the one-sidedness our daily adaptations demand of us. Understood from this angle, the dream raises still more questions.
Do we ever really leave our childhood home? Or rather, does our
primal experience there stay with us and influence, haunt, our
contemporary choices? Is Celine's mother's spirit there in some
palpable way? Or is it her absence now that constitutes the haunting presence? Why would either occasion fear in the dreamer?
And why would one not be apprehensive about these inexplicable
mysteries? Is it the mother's absence that now makes it fearsome
for the dream-ego to cross a threshold and step into the larger
world outside?

Some people only feel liberated in their own life, find permission to stretch and fly, when their parents pass away. Others feel
anxious because, with their parents gone, there is no "home" now.
As Robert Frost said once, home is where you go and they have to
take you in. What if there is no *there* there, no one to take you in?
Is the larger world outside emptier or freer? Is that empty space
"the openness of Being," as Martin Heidegger (1889–1976) suggested, or is it the void, the swallowing abyss? Will the dreamer
be able to step into that largeness that waits outside? Did it in fact
take the passing of the mother to oblige this step, this necessary
prelude to a larger life?

Clearly Celine is at a liminal moment in her life (*limen* means "threshold" in Latin). But threshold to what—abandonment and terror, or freedom and the ticket to her own life, finally? Or maybe it is both. It remains to be seen how this will play out in her life. In the life of every girl, the mother remains a huge figure. After all she is the source, the model, the thing to be emulated, but how, in any particular setting, does this primal ratio play out? One woman said to me recently, "I had to build my model of motherhood alongside of the ruins of the house to which my mother used the wrecking ball of her narcissism."

In the face of any compelling message we have three tendencies. First we are inclined to serve the message, repeat it, identify with it, and replicate it—the more so as the model operates unconsciously within. The second most common reaction is to react against the model and its explicit and implicit messages. "I will be anything but like my mother," except that one is still being defined by that other rather than by the unfolding possibilities that lie within each of us. The third response is to spend one's life trying to "treat" the message. These people live in denial, perhaps generating frenetic activity to distract its thrumming beat upon their souls, or perhaps drugging its interruptive urgencies, or, if truly troubled, they become therapists and try to treat others with similar issues. No matter what strategy one has been driven to elect, one is never free of the power of the model and its message, and never fully freed of its continued invisible work in our lives unless and until it becomes fully conscious. How could one ever choose freely if one is not aware of all of the forces at work in the choices of one's life? This is why Jung suggested that we do not ever "solve" these core problems, but we may out grow them.

For example, the weight and measure of the mother in a daughter's life may be a powerful agency enabling the daughter to live her own life if the mother has in fact lived hers. With all our blunders, the mess we all make of things, the most positive influence can be the authentic life the parent provides the child. This message opens up her imagination, gives her permission, and frees her to make decisions as well. However, when the mother is blocked, bottled up, living through her children or her role alone, a different sort of message is implanted in her daughter.

When the mother is overly identified with motherhood, the

daughter may have a tendency to be similarly identified. Or she may spend her life saying "anything but that" and be driven off her instinctual foundations to a life of overcompensation. She may even be driven to overidentify with male roles, institutions, or values and lose contact with herself. But the invisible presence of that past inevitably emerges in some way; supportive or sabotaging, it will show up. The past is not past.

So, too, the boy will receive compelling messages from his mother. Is she reliable, consistent, available? If so, he will experience the world as generally stable and likely to meet him halfway. Jung's mother was emotionally unstable, and he later said, "When I hear the word *mother*, I think of the word *unreliable*."[1] How does such a message play out in the life of any boy and his subsequent choice of partners? How did that affect his relationship to his own body, his affective life, his connection to the world of feeling, spirit, inspiration? Did he feel that his job was to find a wounded woman and take care of her, as evidenced by many of my male patients? Or will he distrust women and feel he must control them, avoid them, or figure out a way to keep them continuously happy? He will reflexively, redundantly, be driven by the invisible presence to grant the woman in his life an inordinate power, a power not hers inherently but transferred to her by the weight of the inner imago and whatever load up it carries. Thus he will continue to exhibit controlling behaviors, avoidant behaviors, or compliant behaviors, little guessing the inner, historic source of these compelling agendas. Subsequently, he may grow to resent his partner for reasons unknown to both of them, the unconscious being by definition unknown. Whatever patterns are played out with his partner, he will not be without that primal, subtle presence at all times and in all relationships with women. As poet Walt Whitman said of death, "Dark Mother, always gliding near, with soft feet."[2]

And what then of father?

When Jung approached his cleric father with honest questions of religious enquiry, his father replied that he should simply "believe" and not question. From that exchange, Jung reported that he lost confidence in his father and said, "When I think of the word *Father*, I think of *powerless*."[3] So, we have quite a load: "unreliable" mother and "powerless" father. What else is one to do with one's life, having been delivered those messages, but become a psychologist, or an accountant?

What does the reader think upon hearing the word *father*? Is it possible to approach such a summons without history playing an immense role in one's response? Is one not haunted, so to speak, for good or ill, with the detritus of actual experience or, more likely, the experience as it has been inwardly construed and which has thus become one's de facto story?

For some, unlike Jung's complex, the idea of the father will be synonymous with power, for either benevolent or malevolent ends. For some it will occasion a generative source; for others the abuse of power. The poet Gerard Manley Hopkins metaphorically responds to the creation as that which "fathers forth" (p. 2). For some of my patients, the father offers sustaining support, guidance, and empowerment, while for others father is a monster who eats his children out of his own anger, insecurity, and infantile jealousies.

For the initial years of our lives, the father is at times almost irrelevant, so bound is the child to his or her mother. But from about age six through twelve, the father provides the bridge out of the mother/child fusion and creates the necessary tension of the third. Without that third, the child remains bound to the mother. How many three-hundred-pound tackles raise their hands and say "Hi, Mom" on television, and where is Dad in all of that? With more and more fathers missing in action for so many reasons, especially in minority and urban families, the bridge for boys into the adult world is often missing and is more likely to be supplanted either by dependencies, on the one hand, or by a transference to forms of pseudo-adult empowerment such as peer groups and gangs on the other.

Fathers can hardly fulfill their archetypal role if they themselves have not been fathered. How can a man pass on to his children what he has not himself been given? So, we transform our colleges into holding tanks for confused adolescents, swimming in the arms of alma mater, looking desperately for the empowering father who might authorize their lives and validate their journeys, their curiosities, their individuation necessities. So many youth are haunted by the missing gravitational pull of the father, up and out of the mother world, but since one can hardly rail at the darkness, few ever grasp the profundity of that missing piece in their psychic puzzles.

Possibly the most subtle haunting of our lives is the unfinished business of the past. I say this neither to judge nor devalue our ancestors. We have access to information, models, and most of all "permission" to ask questions, take risks, and pursue an individual path, which would have been unthinkable to our predecessors. Still, we all must heed the challenge Jung posed when he noted that the greatest task every child must bear is the unlived life of the parents. Moreover, he believed that he, and perhaps most of us, are

> under the influence of things or questions which were left incomplete and unanswered by . . . parents and grandparents and more distant ancestors. It often seems as if there were an impersonal karma within a family which is passed from parents to children. It has always seemed to me that I had to answer questions which fate had posed to my forefathers, and which had not yet been answered, or as if I had to complete, or perhaps continue, things which previous ages had left unfinished.[4]

Jung's insight is profound, and we need to be reminded of it over and over again. Does not the Bible explicitly say that the "sins" of the fathers are passed on to the children unto the third generation? Did not the great tragedians intimate that some ancestor had offended the gods, who in turn placed a curse upon the house, which then played out in subsequent generations until some heroic figure, through suffering and sacrifice, broke through to an enlarged consciousness and lifted the curse of the haunting? Do not therapists continuously encounter not only the ghostly appearance of the parents in their patient's lives and, implicitly, the presence of the grandparents who similarly formed the complexes, lived the unanswered questions, and generated the models and charged imagoes for the parents as well?

As therapists, when we treat a man who can only express his sexuality when he is high, then we are most likely dealing with a parental inhibition, a complex, a constrictive or punitive message that separates this man from his nature. When we have a woman unable to voice her deepest angers, hopes, and desires, we have some constrictive possession, some febrile haunting. Sometimes these hauntings are so deeply systemic in the person's history that he or she will be unconscious of their presence and will assume that "this is the way things always are" or "this is who I really am" or "how could it ever be otherwise?" Gaining permission is the implicit task: permission to be who one is, permission to serve what wishes to enter the world through us, permission to desire what one most deeply desires, permission to serve the present hour, but permission is equally opposed by the spectral presence of the charged imago, the complex.

Before going further, we need to reexamine, reappropriate, and appreciate anew the radical gift Jung provided us through the idea of the complex. Of all his insights, the complex is perhaps the most practical of his gifts. There is not a single therapeutic hour when I do not think about complexes, recognize their presence, and realize that we are always struggling with compelling spectral presences that have the power to usurp and manage this present hour, and to subvert all the possibilities of this moment into replicative history.

We do not rise in the morning, look in the mirror while brushing our teeth, and say to ourselves, "Today I will do the same stupid things, the reflexive things, the regressive things which I have been doing for years!" But more often than not we indeed do the same stupid, reflexive, regressive things, and why?

Notes
   1. C. G. Jung, *Memories, Dreams, Reflections*, ed. Aniela Jaffé (New York: Pantheon Books, 1961), 8.
   2. Walt Whitman, "When Lilacs Last in the Door-yard Bloom'd." Accessed at http://www.poetryfoundation.org/poem/174748.
   3. Jung, *Memories, Dreams, Reflections*, 8.
   4. Ibid., 233.

CHAPTER 4

Hauntings as Complexes

... We drag

expensive ghosts
through memory's
unmade bed.

—PAUL HOOVER, "THEORY OF MARGINS"

A little over a century ago, Carl Jung was finishing his medical degree at the University of Basel. As he neared the end, he chose as the subject for his medical thesis, the strange case of a medium who allegedly communicated with the shades of the dead. What a strange topic for a physician, both then and now.

In this work he studied a woman who entered into somnambulistic states of suspended consciousness during which the "voices" of the departed spoke through her in forms which were reported recognizable as the voices of the departed. Was she a fraud? Was she psychotic? What did she have to gain, if anything? What Jung did not reveal in this 1902 thesis titled, "On the Psychology and Pathology of So-called Occult Phenomena," was that the subject of his study was his own cousin Hélène Preiswerk, whom he knew personally and whose good faith he trusted.[1] In considering her strange talent, Jung concluded that she had an extremely labile ego state, such as anyone might have who is highly intuitive, drunk, fatigued, or stressed, during which dissociated parts of her own psyche exercised a measure of autonomy and expression. If we think of some of our dreams as examples of how different characters can embody different aspects of ourselves, or how we might, in moments of stress or altered consciousness, say things we might regret or repudiate the next day,

39

then we realize how dissociated aspects of ourselves may in fact rise from our own mouths. To identify those dissociated energies Jung borrowed the term *complex*, which had been coined by a Berlin psychiatrist named Theodor Ziehen (1862–1950) in the previous decade.

When Jung was posted to the Burghölzli, still today the psychiatric hospital of the University of Zürich, he was asked by the director Eugen Bleuler (1857–1939) to explore the so-called word association experiment for its possible usefulness as a diagnostic tool.[2] (The protocol was called an "experiment" rather than a "test" as there is no "right" answer to its stimulus words.) The subject was presented with a series of words to observe his or her reactions. As Jung explored this instrument he found that in supposedly normal subjects, ordinary words were quite capable of producing intrapsychic effects in people. In time he identified more than a dozen indications that disturbances of consciousness occurred, suggesting that the stimulus word had hit some unconscious material within these normal subjects. We all have reactions of various kinds to the stimuli that life brings us. Such reactions occur because we have a history, a psychoactive history, which is reactive, charged, and always present with an affective quantum of energy.

The word *Komplex* in German is a neutral word, as in "an apartment complex" or "an airport complex," namely, a structure, neutral in itself but triggering slightly different meanings to each of us, depending on the variegations of our history. Remember that Jung said when he heard the word *mother* he thought *unreliable* and when he heard *father* he thought *powerless*. Where did he come by these associations other than by having had a history in which these entities were loaded up with valences?

Back when I was teaching in college I used to demonstrate a complex by walking into class and calmly saying, "Please take out a piece of paper and a pen." While the request and its images are essentially banal, students' hearts would seize up and they would be flooded with anxiety. Why? Because who has not been threatened by surprise exams? While my sentence was quite ordinary, the history it activated was not. And beneath the level of the pop quiz anxiety lies a far deeper, archetypal need—the need to feel approved by the other, the need to feel safe, the need to be protected. All of this material is activated by this most ordinary of sentences: "Please take out a piece of paper and a pen." Now we understand what a complex is, and how the present moment is always like a lily pad floating on a vast ocean of affect.

Since a complex has a quantum of energy, charged by history, it always manifests in the body, perhaps as a constriction of the throat, a flutter in the solar plexus, tightening of the muscles, and it always floods the moment with an extra charge of affect. The problem is that in the moment, under the spell of the complex, we usually feel the level of affect generated is appropriate to the moment. Later we might wonder, "Why did I get so upset with my partner last night?" Folk wisdom recognized complexes long before we had a name for them. "Write the letter but don't send it for a few days," and, sure enough, when it comes to sending the letter we do not feel so strongly about the matter.

Most insidiously, a complex has the power to usurp the ego, plunder ordinary consciousness in the moment, oblige us to look through the regressive lens of history, and therein respond to this new moment, this new situation in an old way. Sometimes complexes are protective. We do need to run from some threats; we do need to look both ways before crossing the street; we do need to adapt to circumstances beyond our control. And some complexes help us relate to the new in a grounded way. If one never experienced moments of relational constancy and trust, then he or she would not be able to form relationships. If one has repeatedly experienced betrayal and disappointment from others, most likely he or she cannot value justice, equality, or good faith negotiations. If one has been punished for experiencing beauty, then he or she might cringe before a painting or flee the irresistible affect generated by Beethoven's Ninth Symphony. So, complexes per se are neither good nor bad. What matters is how they play out in our lives. Or, very pragmatically, *what do they make us do or what do they keep us from doing?* To what degree, and in what specific moments of choice, does history govern? Thus, what is most troubling about complexes is their capacity to remove a discriminating judgment from this moment of consciousness, assert, even impose, a historic view generated from an earlier, more likely disempowered place in our history.

Observing someone lying on a couch talking about Mom and

Dad has become such a cliché that only the *New Yorker* continues to approach it in cartoons. But stop and think: what are more
primal messages about self and other, and relational dynamics
between, than our first and most sustained experiences of relat-
edness, especially when we are tiny, vulnerable, and incapable of
comparative analysis? The term Jung used to describe the experience of a complex was *Ergriffenheit*, the state of being seized or
possessed. In other words, when a complex hits, whether benign
or malign in its effect upon us, we are seized by history, possessed
by the past. In such moments we are led to choices that produce
patterns, repetitions driven by the spectral influences of our history, and serving for good or ill to bring about the same old, same
old. No, we do not stand before the mirror in the morning and
say, "Today I will do the same stupid, self-defeating things I have
done for decades." But by day's end, we will have, predictably,
done exactly that.

Try telling a person in the grip of a complex, exhibiting rage,
anxious obeisance, or avoidance, that he or she is in one and they
will not only deny your assertion but most likely have a ready jus-
tification. In fact, one may safely say, in a pseudo-scientific theo-
rem: *wheresoever ready rationalizations exist, thereunto a complex
is being protected.* Thus we are all, much of the time, prisoners of
history, haunted by the spectral "instructions" that float up from
the past to inform, color, dictate our choices in this new present.
This moment is always new; it has never existed before, but we
reflexively, repetitively bind our days, sometimes in moments of
necessary continuity and sometimes in regressive obeisance to
the past. Such is the power of complexes.

By now the reader is surely crying out for an end to theory and
description and hoping for an illustration. Let me respond with
an example that occurred at four p.m. this very afternoon. I ask
the reader to trust the veracity of my report, even as I thank the
analysand for his willingness to share this example with you. He
understood the moment he had the dream what, in general, it
meant and why it had come, and we were both awed by its wisdom and critique of the central complex of his life.

The primary reason we pay attention to dreams is that they
do not arise from the ego. If the reader thinks otherwise, please
try to order up a certain kind of dream tonight with the authority

with which you might order from a restaurant menu and see if the unconscious pays a whit of attention to you. So, here is the dream the analysand, Geoffrey, brought and the situation out of which it emerged.

The dreamer is a man in his seventies who faithfully but fruitlessly nursed and protected his alcoholic wife for decades through a long and troubled marriage until she died. A few years later, he began a relationship with another woman who was, in quite different ways, troubled as well. While he sensed the futility of this later relationship, he also felt compassion for her and did not want to let her drift off into some vague nothingness. Then, to compound things, his adult daughter's life fell apart. He spent considerable time, money, and most of all anxiety trying to help her, her children, and her life situation. Finally, she seemed to be back on an even keel, and he could relax a bit. When his daughter hit a very deep trough again, he was prepared to go to visit her in a distant city and take over whatever he could to help manage. While his efforts on behalf of all three women are notable, even noble, much of his life had been defined by someone else's stuff, someone else's pathology. While he professed not to mind the sacrifice that so much of his life had been, his psyche had another view and wished to be heard.

The morning of his last session before flying off to attempt to rescue his daughter one more time, Geoffrey had the following dream. While its power shocked him, and he knew at one level what it meant and why it had come to him, our discussion led to even deeper engagement with what one might call the central complex of his life. Please remember, the dreamer does not consciously invent this dream, yet it is clearly his dream and has come to confront him from some place even larger in his life than that otherwise dominating complex.

My mother has died. She is in a black casket in front of me. My father and others are there, but they are shadows and say nothing and glide away out of sight.

A doctor and I are going to do an autopsy on the body in the casket. I don't want to do it. The doctor says we must do it so someone gets the benefit from it. I assume someone will get the information from this autopsy.

I think, "Why me? Is this too much for a husband but okay for a son?"

The doctor looks like an old-time magician dressed all in black. He has a long rod with which to pry open the casket.

I am afraid of getting a disease from the decayed body. The doctor opens the casket. A woman in a long black dress with puffed shoulders is lying there. She does not look like my mother at any time in my mother's life. The woman looks young, thirty something, and does not look dead. Now I see it is Jolene [his deceased wife].

She moves as though awakening from sleep. Before the doctor can touch her she pushes herself up with her hands so that her upper body is against the lid and facing us. I am thinking it is Jolene, and I don't want her back alive.

The doctor says, "They would be better off to leave them alone." (I assume he means the woman in the casket or people like her.) He moves to kill her with the rod and close the casket. I yell "no" and stop him. I am horrified at the body coming back to life but am more horrified at killing her now, again.

The woman berates the doctor, scolds him, and calls him by condescending names like she knows him well. I am frozen, huddled up, waiting.

She gets out of the casket. She walks away. She says, "I rule here. I'm back."

Now she floats swiftly through the air toward me. She kisses me on the lips and quickly floats away like a dark shadow and disappears. The taste of her kiss on my lips is acid-bitter.

First of all, who would consciously create this stuff? And yet, undeniably, the dream belongs to the dreamer and arises out of his haunted history. The dream was chilling to him, frightening, and yet resonated in such a way that he knew he would never forget it.

The dream begins by demonstrating that the past is never really past. How scary is the admonishment: "I rule here. I'm back." In every man's relationship with the feminine intimate other the field of mother energy will be active and resonant. When the dreamer was a child, his father was kindly and supportive, but the child clearly picked up an assignment to take care of the wounded woman before him. This charged imago undoubtedly played a role, albeit unconsciously, in his selection of a marital partner, the more so as her impairment demanded his faithful allegiance and sacrificial efforts over several decades until her death.

As a result of his entering therapy in the aftermath of his wife's death, the "doctor" part of him, the part requiring and demanding that an autopsy of events transpire, emerged even as his ego consciousness scarcely wished to return to those painful precincts. Thus, we are told, what the father did not do is now left to the son to address. The doctor is also found in his collaborative partnership with the therapist in therapy. Like an old-time magician, they combine to address mysteries and dark places. The dreamer is naturally reluctant to undertake this dissection, for he fears the onset of the old dis-ease, but we are not even allowed such liberty before the mother figure morphs into his former wife Jolene.[3]

In the dream when he realizes that Jolene is not really gone but has come back to haunt him anew, he is horrified and acknowledges what he could barely admit consciously theretofore, namely, that he does not want to walk down that pathologizing path again. But that complex, that archaic agenda, is truly powerful. It mocks him, challenges his analytic efforts, belittles him, and freezes him.[4]

The archaic script: take care of that wounded woman at all costs, even the cost of your own soul, asserts anew: "I rule here. I'm back." Reflect on the power of the ever-living, the vampiric complexes that attach themselves to our souls and leech our spirits away. Her ghoulish kiss, which haunted and repulsed him even hours later when he recounted the dream, is the kiss of death, not of life, not of love and faithful sacrifice. It is the kiss of death that reaches out from the land of the dead to strike the living anew.

Note when this dream came to him—just as he was departing on his mission to rescue a third generation of wounded women. Of course one has compassion for one's spouse, for one's companion, for one's child, but the cumulative price of this lifelong assignment has been huge indeed. Could we not conclude, as a result of this quite dramatic set of images arising from the deep Self and confronting that history, that he at least ought to try to measure the amount of sacrifice he offers to his adult daughter? I write this on the day he has embarked on the familiar rescue mission, and I await a report on the engagement, compulsive or contained as it may prove to be. Next week together we will again take on the powers of this haunting history, a history that never seems to let go, a history that rises from the grave to impose its ghoulish agenda on the present and dictate its dreadful denouements again. How can any of us, in any moment of action, ever be assured of being free of history, wholly conscious, and absent the interpolating presences of ghostly gestures, spectral scenarios?

When we stop and conscientiously consider our life's patterns, especially the self-defeating patterns, the ones that bring harm to ourselves or others, the ones where we are most stuck, we realize that indeed we are the progenitor of most of our problems. So how and why is this troubling contradiction the case? The answer to this conundrum, which surely has troubled, befuddled, perhaps defeated us all at some moment in our lives, is that our ego is in service to powerfully imprinted "messages," some generated by trauma, some by repetitions, some by "readings" of the world around us. Whether accurate or not, those readings provide the text for the fractal scripts to which the fragile ego—in which we invest so much faith and, frankly, overconfidence—is in service. And the more unconscious that ego servitude is, the more autonomous those messages are.

For example, one woman who had experienced traumatic abandonment in her life went through cleaning frenzies in her house whenever her husband went on a business trip. Once, when he was delayed by bad weather, she fantasized that he was dead, and she imagined selling their house and moving several states away to be near their daughter. When he returned, she collapsed in self-disgust and anxious relief, but she had simply been victimized by the spectral presence of a history that set her up for the likely prospect of the inevitability of abandonment. So concerned were they at her reaction that they entered therapy together, during which her husband pleaded that if he should die before her some day, she should see that natural event, the common destination of our separate journeys, not as one more abandonment. He did not wish his mortal state to reinforce the power of her terrible abandonment complex. In similar fashion, a man who had grown up with a missing father and a crack-snorting mother compulsively followed his wife, tracked her phone calls, and fully expected her to betray him or leave him, just as his parents had. Such is the power of history, especially early trauma, which imprints its message upon our brows with such power that we never fully escape its influence.

I have heard so many excoriate themselves for falling back into an old destructive pattern of one sort or another. We have to learn to forgive ourselves for we have such ghostly haunting because we have history, and history writes its message deeply into our neurology and our psychology. In workshops on various subjects I have often asked the question, "Where are you stuck in your life?" Nowhere, in South America, the United States, Canada, Europe, or Russia, has anyone ever asked me, "What do you mean *stuck?*" We all know, quickly and rather surely, where we are stuck. So why is it that we do not get unstuck? We castigate ourselves for being stuck and assemble New Year's resolutions to get unstuck. Part of why we get stuck is that there is a complex blocking our will, our intentionality, at least as strong as our hope for moving forward. Sometimes resolution, intentionality, willfulness, or concerted, sustained effort is enough to get unstuck, and we get through the blockage. Sometimes that is not enough. Why?

What I have learned from depth psychology is that what we see is often a compensation for what we don't see, and the issue that is readily apparent to consciousness is seldom the real issue, that is, it's not about what it is about. If these two premises are accurate—what we consciously see is a compensation for what we don't see and it's not about what it is about—then no wonder life is so difficult and behavioral psychology has so much trouble tracking our disturbances to such hidden places.

What I have found through the years, both as a human being who suffers complexes as readily as the next person, and as a therapist witnessing their sometimes wicked work hour after hour, is that all of our stuck places track back to the twin existential threats to our survival and well-being: abandonment and being overwhelmed. I have written about these twin threats, and our persistent panoply of management strategies elsewhere, so I will be brief here.[5] Metaphorically, an invisible wire reaches down from the stuck point into the archaic field of our psychological history. Wheresoever we experienced *being overwhelmed*, we also acquire coping strategies of avoidance or struggle for dominance and/or proffer compliant behaviors. Wheresoever we experienced *abandonment* in its many forms, we internalized such deficits as definitions of ourselves and wound up either self-sabotaging, or compelled to overcompensatory behaviors to prove our worth, or we manipulated others to support our shaky sense of self, or obsessively sought reassurance from others, from institutions, from substances, and the like. In other words, *the "stuck" places are much less about our dilatory will than the power of haunting history to reach up from below and, through stuckness, "protect" us from reexperiencing the original traumas of history.* In his discussion on the repetition compulsion—the complex that leads us to repeat our wounding history in such stuck ways—Freud speculated that we are not just programmed to repetition, but that at some level we perversely choose it in order to exercise a measure of control. But even more, and paradoxically, that repetition to feel our chosen pain is still preferable to reexperiencing the primal pain anew. Either way we look at such perverse patterns, so contrary to our conscious will, we must acknowledge the haunting power of history.

The diagram detailing the mechanism of the complex (p. 49) might help. Sometimes we can recognize the presence of a complex in the moment of its nefarious coup d'état. For example, sometime we are able to recognize that the energy generated within us is excessive, far in excess of the reality requirements of the situation. The problem with this indication is that while in the grip of the complex, seeing the situation through its historic lens, that disproportionate energy appears appropriate. Only later, with the lens removed, do we recognize its excess. Still, as we reflect on the role of such historic haunting in our lives, we can sometimes realize, in medias res, that we are more charged and charging than necessary and throttle back a bit. In those moments bad decisions *may* be averted, damage limited.

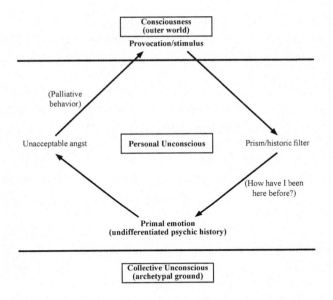

As we all know, often in times of stress or when one's conscious vigilance is reduced, such as through drinking or medication, the protective and inhibitory filters are removed, and the person is prone to rash decisions, including violence. Most domestic violence occurs when the parties are distressed, weakened by drink or substances, or battered by pressures. I have sat in football stadiums and watched ordinary kids turn into violent monsters when caught up in the toxic mix of intractable life frustrations, alcohol, and the anonymity which a crowd seems to promise. Is there, psychologically, a great difference between a rock concert or football match, fueled by booze, pot, and anonymity, and a Nazi rally? One would like to think so, but it is a sobering fact that the human ego consciousness is so easily invaded by complexes, so easily subsumed by the collective sensibility, that ordinary people can be subsumed by collective frenzy. Having undertaken pilgrimages to six former concentration camps, I know the most frightening fact of all of them is that such collective enterprises are made possible not by monsters or psychotics, but by ordinary people caught up in collective complexes and disconnected from a relationship to their own soul. There are not enough monsters in the world to staff those places, provide the transportation, make the round-ups, process the incarcerations, or take the role of neighbors looking the other way. It took the cooperation, both active and passive, of millions to make such horrors happen. In my own country, we are not far removed from justifying the institution of slavery, the extirpation of indigenous civilizations, the segregation of races, the ravishing of the environment, and the sanctioning of torture as an instrument of national policy—all because, once evoked, complexes are replete with justifications aplenty.

When the energy of a complex is activated, it always manifests in the body. The polygraph and many other instruments may measure this discharge of energy and may even tell us things about ourselves of which we are unaware. Sometimes we can catch a complex mid-flight when we feel a familiar distress in the body: sweating or shaky limbs, a flutter in the stomach, a constriction of the throat, and so on. All of these indices are reminders that nothing occurs in the psyche that is not also in the body, since we are one organism; moreover, the body is a powerful register upon which the psyche expresses its calculus of approval or disapproval. It is, for example, a common pathology of therapists, who sit in repose physically, but whose psyches are stressed by the nature of their work, to suffer neck and back disorders. Accordingly, many learn the importance of physical exercise to drain off that energy which the complex has vested in the body, in order to renew both body and spirit for the next day's work.

On some occasions we may see the complex coming, for example, accompanying a forthcoming exam, a medical procedure, or a dental appointment, and plan accordingly. While it is natural to have a measure of apprehension when approaching, for example, a job interview, where much of one's future might be riding on the outcome, how much more difficult the process becomes when the normal stress of such moments is further burdened by, for example, an inferiority complex, a lack of permission complex, or a negative parent complex. I have seen perfectly competent psychoanalytic candidates wash out of training institutes because the negative parent complex is so powerfully constellated that they forget all they know and are reduced to history's frightened child.

Periodically, some polling agency which is having a slow day decides to query the public as to its greatest fears. Over and over, the outcome is the same. The number one fear is not death, not terrorism, but public speaking. Why? We have all experienced the existential task of pleasing "the large other." While that other was once a parent or guardian upon whom our survival and well-being did indeed depend, such an archaic imago, or complex, gets transferred to the amorphous other embodied in an audience.

As one who is profoundly introverted yet who travels and speaks to audiences a great deal, I have learned to deal with this by talking through the complex in advance. I do this in two ways. First, I remind myself to not allow the complex to load up the situation. "These folks are not here to see or judge you. They are here to find help in living their lives. If you have learned anything that may be shared, it will help them do that. That is why they are here, not you!" I really do privately say that to myself. And second, and this is dangerous, I kick a sleeping dog in the basement. I remind myself that I come from a family that was oppressed by lack of education, opportunity, permission to speak out in this world, and that I, their child and grandchild, now have that possibility, so I can speak on behalf of those who could not speak. That puts enough fire in the belly to overcome stage fright. In reality, I invoke a complex to stand up against still another, constricting, complex.

Both strategies are attempts to anticipate the complex, for, like the shark in *Jaws*, it is always circling below, waiting to strike in a thoughtless moment. In the first strategy, I walk out of the complex by reframing its limiting perspective. The new moment is almost always larger and replete with more possibility than the constrictive purview of the past. In the second strategy, I use one complex to take on another. While it can be dangerous business to invite those sleeping dogs to come snarling out of the basement, the old injustices, the shame and denial, have much more power than the anxieties of this present moment. As a result, people have repeatedly said, "This must be easy for you, you seem so calm." But the real battles of our lives are almost always within and were waged long before arriving at that podium.

The central problem is the enormous energy from which core complexes draw their power. Whatever is first, or most archaic, in our history will often draw upon a vast reservoir of energy. Second, consider the limited imagination of such spectral presences. The purview of a complex always is limited to the time and place of its origin. It can only say what its looping tape has to say, hence our self-defeating patterns, the places where we seem unable to avoid bringing harm to ourselves or others. Fortunately, we grow, gain resilience, and learn other possibilities and thereby are more empowered to take on the tasks of the new moment. But we can never presume that the complex, with its ready agenda of regression, will not grab hold of our leg and pull us under. It is often the work of our lives to grow larger than the constrictive arena in which complexes would have us play. When we make such presences conscious, we must conclude that being bound to the past is not acceptable, and we perforce are thrust into a serious fight to recover a larger measure of personal sovereignty.

Charles grew up with an emotionally invasive mother and a passive and ineffectual father. He finally escaped the tyranny of this impossible situation by what I have called "the Seattle solution," namely, he moved as far away from his family of origin as he possibly could without drowning in the sea. But we travel with our suitcases filled with history, and there, just beneath the underwear and socks, that history waits to be replayed in the new setting. Accordingly, unaware as he was of the power of this constellating complex, his radar found and married an emotionally troubled woman, and he quickly became as dominated by her distresses as he had been by his mother. To "solve" this problem he turned first to depression (anger turned inward and learned helplessness), then to self-medication of the depression through alcohol, then to an affair with a woman two hours drive away. Their brief trysts were governed by his guilt—which is to say anxiety from violating his good-boy complex—and ended by making both Charles and his mistress miserable.

Because the relationship of the child to the invasive parent is so large, Charles seemingly has only two options: obey it and be depressed, or violate its script, which causes huge anxiety and attendant guilt. His task is to be angry neither with his mother nor his wife, her surrogate, but with the constrictive power of the complex that reigns in sovereign tyranny and to figure out what he really wants to do with his life. Living either in obeisance to, or revolt from, the powerful other is a poor way to conduct a life. Figuring out his own journey, his own desire, sounds easy enough, but it is exceedingly difficult to achieve, given the power of the primal message that his psychological reality did not count, and given that his well-being lay in being adaptive and subordinate to the narcissistic needs of others.

We all have these, or similar, archaic instructions. They have been around so long we simply have grown familiar with them, like bad habits. But *we are not our history*; ultimately, *we are what wishes to enter the world through us*, though to underestimate the power of that history as an invisible player in the choices of daily life is a grave error. Further examples of the activity of these spectral presences provides the grist of the next chapter, and then we will turn to how we might break the bonds of these spectral presences in our lives.

Notes

1. C. G. Jung, "On the Psychology and Pathology of So-called Occult Phenomena" (1902), in *Psychiatric Studies*, vol. 1, *The Collected Works of C. G. Jung* (Princeton, NJ: Princeton University Press, 1957).

2. C. G. Jung, "The Association Method" (1909), in *Experimental Researches*, vol. 2, *The Collected Works of C. G. Jung* (Princeton, NJ: Princeton University Press, 1973).

3. In the third of R. M. Rilke's *Duino Elegies*, on the nature of love, he explores how when one embraces the other the archetypal realm, the personal history, and multiple ancestral personages are involved in that embrace. When we embrace the other, history is present in each gesture, each enacted script, each outcome. Accessed at http://www.poetryintranslation. com/PITBR/German/Rilke.htm#_Toc509812217.

4. We all have primal fears which, when evoked, freeze and paralyze. There is an inner Medusa in each of us which turns us to stone when we stare into her pitiless eyes. Shakespeare described the power of such complexes over four centuries ago when he confessed how often "resolution is sicklied o'er with the pale cast of thought . . . and lose the name of action" (*Hamlet*, act 3, scene 1).

5. See James Hollis, *Finding Meaning in the Second Half of Life: How to Finally, Really Grow Up* (New York: Gotham Books, 2006), 46–64.

CHAPTER 5

Our Danse Macabre

Relational Ghosts, Relational Hauntings

At some point in grade school our teacher played a haunting piece of music for us. At the time I did not remember the name of the composer, Saint Saëns, but I never forgot the title, as she explained it to us: *Danse Macabre.* The *Totentanz* or dance of death, was a familiar motif in medieval iconography, church ritual, and popular culture. Soon, very soon, the ineluctable message: Master Death will arrive, and all of us, irrespective of class or station in life or moral record, will dance to his piping into the gaping grave. How often later in life, as a therapist, I have thought on that metaphor, how often I have observed the relational patterns of thoughtful, well-intentioned people, who seemed pulled irresistibly by the spectral presences of the past into the seductive graves of diminished choice. How often they seem compelled without pity by energies that led them to old places, familiar dead ends, and wounding arenas. Perhaps the best way to illustrate this troubling phenomenon is by providing some examples of dreams, the memorable way the psyche illustrates what is really going on. Recall that our ego state does not create our dreams, but they are our dreams nonetheless. So some energic source within each of us is observing, invested, and offering a commentary to whomever may be able to hear. My clients have provided some notable examples through the years, examples graphically depicted in the narratives which arise from our psyches each night, revealing to us our various homages paid to the dead past. The dead, it seems, are not dead and dance on still.

Earlier today, I spoke with Denise, a mature woman who has lived a thoughtful, productive professional life but was undone once again by the prospect of visiting her city of birth because she would have to spend time with her father. The father dominated the sons and daughters of the family, obliged them to serve his needs, and drove them always toward accomplishments so that he might feel better about his own wretched life. While they lived in relative affluence and privilege, the inner life of the father was, and remains, impoverished. So he demands of his adult children obeisance, flattery, and servitude. My client, wishing to return to that city and spend time with friends and siblings, knew that she would have to tell her father the truth, namely, that being with him, serving his needs, was an impossibly high price of visiting. Yet to say these words understandably occasioned enormous anxiety in her. While she would not permit anyone else to treat her with the disdain and control her father wielded, the price of saying no to him remained daunting and disabling.

Again, recall that our psyche metaphorically is an analogue computer, asking have I been here before, what was the message of that experience, and what is my best course of action here? This process occurs in an instant, as a reflex, and our ego state is momentarily flooded by the data of that earlier time and circumstance. To the child within each of us, the parent remains always a giant with gigantic powers to help or hurt. That deeply programmed imago is never left behind, and carries with it a large charge of energy, a waiting script, and a predictable outcome. While it might seem simple to the outsider to say to the father, "I have had enough of this control and manipulation, and this is how I plan to spend my time while visiting, and you may have only this much of it," to approach that abyss is to open up the spectral presence of the past and to experience unacceptable levels of anxiety. But at least in Denise's case we are not in doubt as to where the stress is coming from. We are not in denial concerning the real feeling life, the desire for personal freedom, of the daughter.

Jeremy, a sixty-something man, confessed remorse at having lashed out at his wife. Her attentiveness to his efforts around the house had resulted in his screaming at her to leave him alone. So exaggerated was his reaction that they both knew it was not about the situation at hand—it was about the spectral presence of the past. His mother was invasive, frequently prying into his childhood in painful and embarrassing ways. She was convinced that if one did not have a full bowel movement every day, one would die of toxicity, and so into his high school years, she demanded to examine his daily productions to assess his health. It was not until he finally went away to college that he learned that one did not have to have a bowel movement every day, and that if one did not, one would not suffer a debilitating illness. Traveling home at spring break, he strapped a javelin to the car so that he could practice his track event. When the force of the wind blew away the towel he had used for padding, he stopped in a panic. His passenger asked him why, and he replied with great anxiety, "She has all the towels counted, and if I am one short, she will scream at me." When they returned to campus after the break his companion told this story to others, and soon Jeremy became the butt of the dorm's teasing: "Did you count your towels today?" "Did you get a good shit today?" and so on. The shame and worthlessness he felt abides with him today. So when his wife looks in on him, he jumps down her throat. He and I know why, and now his wife knows why, but he cannot help himself from having this excessive reaction.

Both of these persons are extremely competent, capable individuals, and both came to know not only the nature of these core complexes, which were running their lives, but also the corrective, redemptive efforts of the Self to bring enlargement and healing to them. Both had dreams that helped them gain a perspective larger than the ego, beleaguered as it was, and both came to recognize that the dreams were theirs, that they had come from some place outside the ego frame as their friend, their advocate, their mentor.

Denise, anxiety ridden by the forthcoming visit to her city of origin, dreamed that she was met at the airport by the mayor of the city, who, in a solemn ceremony, welcomed her home and told her she had brought great honor to the city. Her father, present at this ceremony, simply walked away, perhaps dismayed that he was not the center of the occasion. While the dreamer felt a flash of nostalgia in the dream for her departing father, she also knew that it was important for her to be present to the mayor and to be honored. The mayor in the dream was not the current mayor of her city, but a more famous mayor of her childhood.

She understood that he embodied a more objective view of her, a celebratory affirmation of her worth, having nothing to do with the father. While she felt sad for her mother, she knew that she was being asked to define herself as someone other than the person defined by her father's narcissistic needs. After all, if the famous mayor, perhaps a surrogate for the Self, saw her worth, who was the father, or the dreamer, to argue with him?

Jeremy, hypersensitive to his wife's observant presence, dreamed a series of dreams, the most traumatic of which was one in which his mother came screaming at him like a banshee, trying to swallow him in her open mouth. He compared the image to a shrieking face from the painting *Echo of a Scream* by Mexican artist David Siqueiros (1896–1974). Another dream featured his wife, wearing the clothing common to the fifties when he was a child, and a set of cereal boxes that he treasured as a child. On the back of these cereal boxes were cowboys and heroic figures whose exploits were compensatory to his enslaved condition. During this stage of his life he had saved up pennies and nickels to send off for magic rings, spy glasses with codes, and costumes of these mythic saviors. His youthful psyche was desperately hungering for male energies and these cardboard hero figures offered themselves up to him in appealing forms.

All relationships, *all relationships*, involve two elemental psychological mechanisms at all times: *projection* and *transference*. The only question is the degree to which these mechanisms operate unconsciously and, as a result, make us do certain things or keep us from doing certain things. In Jeremy's dream we see that he has projected onto his wife something of the power of the mother imago. How could he not? His mother was quite simply the most important woman he had ever met, especially given her omnipresence and omnipotence during his most formative years. Now his wife is ostensibly the most important woman in his life, but inevitably he projects the power of that earlier woman onto his partner and transfers to her a power that she does not have in reality. But once one looks at the other through the lens of the past, that power and its attendant strategies are transferred to the new person, the new moment, but with the agenda, the script, and the predictable outcome of the first go around.

As an aside, in speaking to women's groups about men, I define and illustrate this transference phenomenon in relationships and declare that it forces the man to grant the woman too much power in his life. While this bestowal of power might seem flattering at first, it is based on an unreal relationship, a relationship defined not by the man's reality-based engagement with his wife but by history. Given that the woman has received this inordinate power, the man is set up to have only three choices: keep her happy at all costs, try to control her, or avoid her as much as possible. Many of the women in these groups pipe up: "My husband does all three." While "keeping her happy" may be exploited by an unconscious or devious wife, it operates not out of loving concern but out of power. Macho behavior is a telling indication of the magnitude of the transferred power of the mother imago. The more a man swaggers, the more insecure he is in his own masculine nature. (This is why homophobia is an unwitting confession by macho types of the hidden power of the feminine, and why it is most pronounced among macho assemblies such as sports teams or the military where one needs to define one's self in male constructs on a daily basis simply to hold one's ground.) Similarly, male avoidance of intimacy is in direct proportion to what degree the man felt invaded in his childhood. Accordingly, virtually all adult relationships are ghostly reenactments of earlier times and places, earlier personae, and earlier scripts.

Jeremy's dream was so clear: his wife in the clothing and setting of childhood. How could one not see this sinister connection? It would be tempting to report that these dreams led people to vanquish the diminishing power of the past overnight. They did not. But for both Denise and Jeremy, the dreams seemed to objectify another kind of energy that was rising to inform, support, and perhaps heal them. For Denise, the mayor himself says she is of great value, has brought honor to her city, and has nothing to do with her father in all this. For Jeremy, his partner is the unfortunate carrier of the debris of an unresolved past. Because he loves his wife, because he wants to be a free man, because he wishes to claim his own life journey, Jeremy today is much more self-contained, much more in the present. Occasionally, he will flash back at his wife, but they both recover quickly, knowing that it is not about them, but about someone long ago and far away. It is difficult to remember this in the heat of the moment, but the more we can remember, the greater the purchase on the present moment. Thus the wisdom of Edmund Burke, repeated in George Santayana's observation, that those who do not learn from the past are condemned to repeat it. This truth plays out not only on national stages as presidents and pontiffs parade their neuroses at the expense of the rest of us, but in the most intimate of chambers as well. In fact, the more intimate the relationship, the more present the dramas of the past, for they mean more to us, cost us more, and therefore carry the heaviest freight.

Let me illustrate the spectral *danse macabre* with two more examples, again using dreams as the point of entry.

Ilse had been born into an old European family where the paterfamilias exercised a benevolent dictatorship, choosing her friends and her values for her. Her mother was a passive participant in this protective regime. Naturally he would have denied that he played a domineering role, arguing that all he ever did was see to the best for his daughter, and Ilse wholeheartedly subscribed to this reading of their relationship. At the onset of World War II, the family emigrated to America, and Ilse entered the same scientific profession as her father. She married only when her father was dying; and the man she chose, Karl, was a generation older and in the same profession. She considered this marriage idyllic and she did not know that she had merely handed the baton of authority to the next intimate male, external other in her marital choice. It was not that she was "marrying her father," but she was surely wed intrapsychically to what she experienced as the benevolent role of the father complex, along with its attendant authority. She entered therapy at age sixty-five, when she was widowed by the death of her husband.

While her grief was real, and understandably the focus of the therapy initially, Ilse steadfastly resisted remembering her dreams, claiming first that she never dreamed and later that only vague images hovered over her waking moments before slipping back into the unconscious. While her professional life was one of considerable achievement, her flight from the summons to personal authority persisted in her resistance to the idea that an authority might be found within. She had a strong positive transference to her therapist and expected him to tell her what to do with her life now as she faced both retirement and widowhood. It was several months into the therapy when she reported her first full dream, and I knew the moment she spoke it aloud that we had moved from a legitimate process of grief work to an analytic frame.

Karl and I are on some sort of pilgrimage together and are walking side by side. As we reach a flowing stream, I realize that I have forgotten my purse and must go back and fetch it. Karl goes ahead. I return to our car, retrieve my purse, and return to the path we were on. When I reach that bridge again and begin to cross, a man my age, but unknown to me, joins me from the left and we begin to talk.

I understand at this moment that Karl is both just ahead of me, and that he is also dead. I tell this stranger about my loss, my terrible bereavement, and then, to my shock, he says to me, "I know, I understand, and it has been good for me!" [referring to himself].

Ilse certainly understood that she and her husband Karl had been on a journey together, that in some way they still were, though he has gone ahead of her, but she was puzzled by the symbol of the missing purse and offended by the insensitive, even cavalier, attitude of the stranger who averred that her suffering was good for "him."

After all these years, and so many dreams, I have seen hundreds of missing purses. What does one carry in a purse: personal effects, even, one might say, one's personality, confirmation of identity, resources, keys, capital, and many other things. It is never a good thing to lose one's purse. Ilse had left these things behind in Europe many decades before, or better, had folded them into the protective but constrictive embrace of the father/daughter symbiosis.

The stranger is somehow a familiar companion to her, of the same age, for he has been around exactly as long as she has, but he is a stranger to her conscious life. Yet the psyche brings the two together on that fateful bridge of transition, a crossing over into a different stage of the journey and demanding a more reflective psychology to direct it. In classical Jungian terms, the stranger is her animus, the so-called inner masculine that had been enfolded so long in the father complex that she had never known her personal authority. As long as her life flowed in its protected way, she had only the easy decisions to make, and she made them with professional skill and alacrity, but when it came to the question of who she was and what she stood for, she was still a sweet child on history's large and indifferent stage. Only the suffering occasioned by the removal of the protective blanket of well-meaning males in her life could lead her to this crossroads. This is why the stranger, who is strange only to ego consciousness but who has always been with her, says that her suffering was good for him, that is, because it made their conscious encounter with each other possible.

Ilse's attitude toward the stranger and the task he brought her was more than ambivalent; she disavowed the summons that the integration of this animus energy asked of her. A woman's encounter with the negative animus is usually embodied as self-denigration: "What makes you think you can do that?" The positive animus is experienced as not only the capacity to take who one is *into* the world, but the permission to do so. Such an energy has a gravitas, a grounding, and an empowering effect on a woman's life. Given that the primary task of the second half of life is the recovery of personal authority, namely, to discern what is true for oneself and find the courage to live it, Ilse was being summoned in this dream to grow up and be her own adult. From all outward parameters, she was very much an adult, and a productive one as well, but from an inner perspective, she was only now, at sixty-five, taking on the true mantle of adult accountability.

She hated that stranger and his insensitivity to her loss, and even more, the summons he brought her to integrate the life-expanding energy he embodies into her life. To her credit, Ilse took on this project and over the years made a great number of changes to her life, all based on risking a personal authority which theretofore had not been available. In time, she even left the church of her tradition and became a Quaker, doubly significant because of the Quaker emphasis on accessing divine guidance not through priests, hierarchies, or vested authority but through trusting an inner light. Her shift of religious affiliation was a signal of her taking on the project of personal authority and wresting it from the benevolent but spectral presence of the father.

Damon was a thirty-six-year-old British graduate student of German language and literature. He was in Zürich completing a

PhD with the expectation of returning to England to teach at the collegiate level. His presenting issues were a persistent depressive affect, feeling always that he was on the periphery of his own life, and difficulty sustaining intimate relationships with women. Several weeks into his therapy, he had the following dream, which is set back in England with his family of origin:

We are on holiday and get into our car and leave London. As we drive out into the countryside, we pass a field of peasants or farmers working their crops. I announce to everyone: "That is how real people live!"

We stop at a roadside inn and have lunch and then drive on until the road peters out and we get out and walk into a forest. As we go deeper into the forest, it gets darker and darker, and I feel apprehensive. Then, in the distance, we see the glow of lights and faintly hear music playing. As we draw near, we see it is actually a mansion lit up, and my father says to me, "This is Keats's house." I say, "No, it couldn't be because Keats spent his whole life in and died in London." But my father insists and when we get to the entrance of the mansion, there is a bronze plaque which says, "John Keats's House."

We go inside and some sort of theatrical performance is going on. There are no chairs, so we go to the front and seat ourselves on the floor. I realize that it is an erotic ballet version of Shakespeare's A Mid-Summer Night's Dream. *After awhile one of the dancers, a young woman comes over to me and holds out her hand as an invitation to join the performance as her partner. I am shy and feel uncomfortable but think, "Why not?" We begin to dance together, slowly but closely and purposefully. Then the phone rings and someone tells me it is my mother calling and that we left her stuck in the toilet back at the inn and I am required to go back and fetch her. I am furious that this is taking me away from the dance, but I feel I have no choice and leave.*

The reader may wonder, as I do, how we dream such things. Perhaps we do not fill our dreams with the literary associations of this particular dreamer, but we all do rummage through our own experience and from that detritus form images from the depths which speak to the conduct of our journey. To realize that we have such sources of guidance within is to be assured that we do have a source for personal authority, for guidance and solace, and for a more considered life.

Recall that Damon's presenting issues are the persistent depressive cloud over his life and his ambivalence toward intimacy with women. We all carry our families of origin with us as spectral presences, so this dream begins with the family together as before. As they leave the world of conscious ego construction, the city, they enter into the countryside and less conscious realms. Damon's pronouncement that the farming folk are *real* people reveals his self-critical attitude toward himself as someone unreal, living in his head but not his heart and his body.

When I asked why it was that his father announced that the mansion they encountered was the residence of John Keats, the nineteenth-century poet, Damon replied, "Keats died young. He wrote his own epitaph: 'Here lies one whose name was writ on water.' My father never got to live his life either." "What was his life about, then?" "Taking care of my mother was his whole life." Damon felt that while his father would not have known that information about Keats, he felt his own provisional hold on life was in turn modeled on his father's failure to provide a more dynamic model for a boy to emulate. If Damon believes, as his complex has internalized and now dictates, that his job is to take care of a narcissistically demanding partner, no wonder he is ambivalent about intimacy.

Damon associated the Shakespeare play with joie de vivre, the dance of life, and was astonished that he was in fact invited to join. Overcoming his inhibitions, he takes the hand of this psychopomp, this guiding anima presence, and begins the dance, but alas, the power of the old complex reasserts its sovereignty and pulls him out of this union with its more enriching possibilities. When I asked why the mother was "stuck" in the toilet, he replied that she had always associated the body, and sexuality in particular, with something dirty, surreptitious, and foreign. What a divisive, troubling message to pass on. No wonder he was depressed and estranged. What else could he be when in the grips of this spectral succubus, this denier of life?

These stories are real, the dreams are real, yet the dilemmas each person faces are founded on the presences that haunt from their past. We see again the twin mechanisms present in all relationships: projection and transference. Each of them, meeting any stranger, reflexively scans the data of history for clues, expectations, possibilities. This scanning mechanism is instantaneous, mostly unconscious, and then the lens of history slips over one's eyes. This refractive lens alters the reality of the other and brings to consciousness a necessarily distorted picture. Attached to that particular lens is a particular history, the dynamics, the script, the outcomes of which are part of the transferred package. Freud once humorously speculated that when a couple goes to bed there are six people jammed together because the spectral presences of the parents are unavoidable. One would have to add to this analogy the reminder that those parents also import their own relational complexes from their parents, so we quickly have fourteen underfoot, not to mention the persistence of even more ancestral influences. How could intimate relationships not be congested arenas?

As shopworn as the idea seems, we cannot overemphasize the importance of primal imagoes playing a domineering role in our relational patterns. They may be unconscious, which grants them inordinate power, or we may flee them, but they are always present. Thus, for example, wherever the parent is stuck—such as Damon's mother who only equates sexuality with the perverse and the unappealing, and his father who stands de-potentiated and co-opted—so the child will feel similarly constrained or spend his or her life trying to break away ("anything but that") and still be defined by someone else's journey. How could Damon not feel depressed, then, at his own stuckness, and how could he not approach intimacy with such debilitating ambivalence?

Given that the problem of the unconscious is that it is unconscious, we only become aware of this hidden haunting when we have served it many times and begin to see a pattern, when we have revelatory, compensatory dreams, or when we grow large enough to take on the burden of history that courses through each of us. When we are young, the ego is insufficiently formed to attempt such a massive project. After many years of serving these spectral messages, the ego may have gained sufficient energy, sufficient solidification to undertake such a self-examination. It sounds simple but in fact it is not, for the ego will be required to stand before humbling recognitions, daunting challenges, and intimidating prospects of risk. We say we wish to undertake this project, but normally we only address whatever parts need greater consciousness when our suffering is no longer deniable or manageable. So Denise had to suffer the anxious crisis of necessary choice, Jeremy the disturbance of terrifying dreams, Ilse the deaths of her father and her husband, and Damon the oppression of depression, desuetude, loneliness, and longing. Without that suffering, there is no call to consciousness, no showing up for the appointment we have with life. We all keep slip-sliding away until something catches us and holds us to accountability.

Jung once observed that each therapist must ask the question: What task is this person's neurosis helping him or her avoid? Sooner or later, the necessary path of healing becomes clear. We can no longer avoid the "going through." *Going through* means that that which we have neglected through denial, unconsciousness, or living in *mauvaise foi*, remains as unfinished business. In the book *Swamplands of the Soul*, I noted that in every swampland visitation we experience, there is always a task, the addressing of which can move us from victimage to active participation in the construction of our journey, and the flight from which invariably leads to the same old, same old. Or, as poet Gerard Manley Hopkins put it, to remain our own "sweating selves."[1]

How unpleasant to realize that finally we all have to face what we fear? All of us. How unpleasant to realize that until we do, the life we are living is at least partially in service to the dictates of the past, the persistent, interfering ubiquity of which cannot be exaggerated. Discerning these presences with their urgent, redundant messages is only the first step. But we will not take even that first step until we have to, until it costs too much not to. Even in our brightest moments, the *danse macabre* plays on, for the dead are not dead, nor are they gone. A vast company of ancestral presences embraces us in dance, always. In sundry forms and fashions, they are present always, and their gestural messages move through our limbs and our choices . . . and here we thought we were alone on this journey.

Note
1. Gerard Manley Hopkins, *Poems and Prose*, ed. W. H. Gardner (New York: Penguin Books, 1953), 62.

CHAPTER 6

Guilt Ghosts, Shame Ghosts

Alas, I rather hate myself
For hateful deeds committed by myself.
—WILLIAM SHAKESPEARE, *RICHARD III*, ACT 5, SCENE 5

Recently a man whom I had been counseling for some time came in shattered. His adolescent son had committed suicide, leaving no note, amid no overt symptoms of depression or debilitating conflict. Not only was this father stricken by the loss of his beloved child, he was ridden with guilt: What should I have seen? Did I do something wrong? Did I fail to do something? These questions are initially reasonable and responsible, but their persistence becomes obsessive and lacerating. How many of us are so afflicted by decisions made and not made in our past? And what can one say to a parent in such a moment of extremity?

I tried to make the following points: First, none of us knows the stresses within another person, and often what they do makes sense to them at the time. Even though we feel it a violation of what we consider the natural order of things, to have a child precede a parent, we are all on the same mortal journey together, albeit strung out separately along the way. Second, the loss of a child does change one's world forever, but I would suggest two things: a) talk to the son at least once a day to honor the relationship, knowing that death does not end relationships, and b) consider what values one held in common with the child and continue to serve those values as best we can. Third, in any case, we all have separate lives, separate journeys, separate destinies, and we do not serve those lost by abrogating or sabotaging our own summons to live. Rather, we are reminded to live even more consciously in the face of loss and to treasure what relationships, and what tasks of growth, are still around us. Just how is it that we would serve the child's memory by not showing up in our own lives?

I came to these conclusions the hard way, not as a therapist, but as a parent who lost his child as well. Joining the dismal company of so many grieving parents, the world's worst club, I also suffered guilt, asked all the self-incriminating and lacerating questions, and still do, but I also consider my life both a testament to what we shared so abundantly and as a spur to show up and not be afraid of what life has yet to bring. How I used to puzzle over the terrible admonition of the Greeks: "Not to have been born is best, and to have died young second best." Surely that "wisdom" was too pessimistic. But now I know why they might have so concluded, for to live long is to suffer loss after loss, even while not to live long is to bring loss to others. Moreover, to live long, and perhaps grow more thoughtful, is to have more consciousness, more insight, and, frankly, much, much more about which to feel guilt, or at least complicity. Still, showing up seems important. It was after personal loss that I rediscovered Marcus Aurelius and remembered not to "grumble at setting out to do what I was born for, and for the sake of which I have been brought into the world."[1]

As humans we are gifted by memory and also cursed by it. The memory of sweet moments can serve as a susurrus to the cacophonous timbre of the present. But the memory of trauma can make us adverse to risk, hesitant before the task of the hour, or, having identified with our adaptations to the existential demands of a fortuitous environment, out of touch with our guiding instincts and our capacities for enlargement. We are equally equipped with the prospect of envisioning the future. Such a gift allows us to anticipate the rigors of the journey and the provisions needed, and perhaps even to intuit behind which bush the predator might wait. Nonetheless, the cost of a burdening past is guilt, and the cost of an uncertain future is anxiety. Each affective state, guilt or anxiety, has the capacity to erode our participation in the moment and remove us from instinctual guidance in service to agendas of the past or anticipations of the future. Given that this book is about hauntings, we will focus here on the burdensome powers of the past.

While the capacity to feel guilt makes us sentient, potentially moral, creatures, the weight of guilt is often crippling. Mark Twain once noted that we are the only animal capable of feeling embarrassment, and the one with most legitimate claim upon that emotion. So, too, it may be argued, is our capacity for guilt. And while it is often true, as the surrealist poet Guillaume Apollinaire declared, "memories are hunting horns whose sound dies out along the wind," more often memories haunt us, drain the joy of this hour, and even oblige numbing behaviors, divertissements, and projections of accountability onto others.[2]

Many of our behaviors, conscious and unconscious, are driven by guilt, shame, anxiety, and other dismal denizens of the soul. Typically, guilt shows up in our lives in one of three ways: patterns of avoidance, patterns of overcompensation, or patterns of self-sabotage. Guilt drives us away from the normal attractions of life by feelings of unworthiness. In overcompensating, one seeks to "treat" this unknown disorder by demonstrating one's worth, one's power or wealth, or one's magnanimity (as Pearl Bailey, a great American psychologist, put it, "Thems what thinks they is, ain't"). In the third form, the burden of guilt demands accounting, retribution, payback, and often leads to self-denigration, self-flagellation, or self-abuse before the compelling ledger sheet for things done, things not done, is balanced. (Oedipus, viewing the weight of his unconscious choices, blinds himself and pleads for death, only to be punished even further by exile and long repentance, the burden of guilt and exile being a more exacting punishment than execution.)

When we reflect on the strange paradox that guilt binds us to the past and anxiety to an unknown future, it seems that we might rarely be present to *this* moment, *this* reality, insofar as we are driven by guilt or anxiety. But there is a place for guilt. And what is that place?

To answer that question we have first to recognize that there are at least three modalities of guilt, all with very powerful claims upon our emotional lives. They are:

1. Legitimate guilt as a form of accountability for our choices
2. Contextual guilt
3. Illegitimate guilt as a form of anxiety management

Guilt as Accountability

No matter what the exigencies, the crises of the moment, all philosophical, theological, and psychological systems hold us accountable at the end of our lives for the consequences of our choices,
no matter how well intended they may have been at the moment.
While courts may sometimes recognize a diminished capacity
for making choices, generally we are held before the bar of real
life, real choices, and real outcomes. The night I am writing this
paragraph an Italian captain is being charged with abandoning
his ship and passengers in the moment of peril. How easy it is
to sit in judgment, and judged he must be, even as all of us remember shameful moments of turning away from what we knew
was right, what we knew we were called to confront. An earlier
illustration of this dilemma was depicted by Joseph Conrad in
his novel *Lord Jim*, a fine account of this burden of guilt and the
many ways the central character sought to compensate for his
own panic during a crisis at sea. All of us have vulnerable spots in
our armor, areas of personal vulnerability, and we are fortunate
indeed if the fates do not bring us to those terrible places in our
lives. All of us have some aperture where we are most frightened,
least able to resist the rapid transport which every complex embodies out of this moment into dismal places past.

While technology advances and social contexts vary, human
nature does not. All of the great religious and spiritual observers
have witnessed this tendency in all of us, and they often provide a
form of expiation and renewal. Greek tragedy, for example, was a
highly moral view of the universe in which choice, consequence,
consciousness, guilt, recognition, and compensation unfold.
Those who returned humbled before the gods were redeemed;
those who would not bend the knee of contrition perished. So,
too, rites of expiation, conscious scapegoating, repentance, and
confession were institutionalized and made available to the sincere that they might be renewed and enabled to go on with life.
Others, lacking such beliefs or rites or sacraments are eaten up
with compensatory behaviors, anesthetizing practices, and the
erosion of any participation in the celebration of life.

After consciousness brings accountability, confession, atonement, or compensation is obliged, unless, as the twelve-step

programs recognize, to do so would bring further damage to aggrieved parties. Many times the compensation is not possible without further damage, or at best some symbolic offering is substituted as a symbolic gesture for the loss, injury, or grievance.

If the accountability and confession and compensation are sincere, the possibility of atonement, or becoming one again with oneself, and restored relations with the wounded party may be possible. Underneath this gesture is the notion that we all feel better somehow when living in good faith with the other and with ourselves. The etymology of both *penitentiary* and *reformatory* speak to the human need to feel connected with others again. Sadly, there are of course those so damaged in their relationship with another that such restoration of right relationship is impossible. They remain frozen in sociopathic or schizoid distance from others as a radical form of protection and suffer a fate even worse than the guilt-ridden—they are locked in isolating prisons from which there seems no escape without enduring the overwhelming threat of accountability.

After sincere recognition, recompense, and repentance, one may find the grace of release. I say *grace*, because this fortuitous gift may be experienced even by those most guilt-ridden. Grace is the experience of feeling restored to community with self and with others, apart from whatever one has done or failed to do. Perhaps the best definition of grace came from theologian Paul Tillich who said that grace requires accepting the fact that one is accepted despite the fact that one is unacceptable. This is not something that can be earned—not by money, not by wearing a hair shirt, not by compensatory behavior—but is a gift rising out of the generosity of others.

The ability to own our own guilt, to acknowledge our shadowy capacity for wrong of all kinds, paradoxically allows us to move in new ways into the world. The trick is not to be defined by that guilt and its compensatory or evasive agendas, but to admit the wounds and flaws that characterize our species. Such a person, Jung wrote, now

> knows that whatever is wrong in the world is in himself, and
> if he only learns to deal with his own shadow he has done

something real for the world. He has succeeded in shouldering at least an infinitesimal part of the gigantic, unsolved social problems of our day. . . . How can anyone see straight when he does not even see himself and the darkness he unconsciously carries with him into all his dealings?[3]

As the Roman playwright Terence observed two millennia ago, "Nothing human is alien to me." Ironically, this devastating insight into ourselves is also the key to self-acceptance, to legitimate guilt but also to legitimate reinvestment in life. If I can accept Terence's conclusion, then I may even be able to accept myself—when all of us know how unacceptable a proposition that may prove to be. To accept one's humanity is also to experience the necessity of grace, grace toward others who have wronged us, and even, much more difficult, grace bestowed unto ourselves.

Guilt as Contextual Consciousness

The second form of allegiance to the spectral presences of the past shows up as contextual guilt. As animals coexisting on this spinning globe, we live by killing: other animals sometimes, vegetal life often, and we daily serve the paradox of this life that our lives depend upon the killing of some other living form. We pretty it up with dogmas of superiority, rationalizations of divinity-bestowed rights, and whatever ploys necessary to preserve the fragile stability of the ego. It is not sentimentality to see that the great systole-diastole of life is the life-death dialectic of which we are an active and compromised part. Our ancestors finessed this paradox not only with stories of innate superiority but with rituals which divinized killing, submitting the various acts of violence to a divine drama, the "cycle of sacrifice" as I called it in *Tracking the Gods: The Place of Myth in Modern Life*. Thus, they offered "grace" as a form of thank you and expiation for the slaying of the other. Today, we deal with it by distancing ourselves from the slaughter that goes on around us, not only of sentient beings but of forms of life that we increasingly find also have natural "intelligence," even primitive types of consciousness. So it has been, so it will be. It is moral obtuseness not to observe this daily fact rather than rationalize it away and accuse others of pathological sensitivity. A former vice president of the United States was lampooned for speaking out on behalf of the planet, even though it is clear the ecological balance of the planet is increasingly in jeopardy and will have the final say.

Even more, those of us privileged to live in the so-called first world live on the backs of children and exploited adults throughout the rest of the world. When Candide set off on Voltaire's magical mystery tour in the seventeenth century, he visited the Caribbean where he saw the appalling conditions of work life in the sugar plantations and concluded that now at least he understood the real price of a lump of sugar to sweeten milady's tea in Paris. Once we have tumbled to some form of consciousness around these matters, we have to acknowledge the tennis shoes on our feet, the jeans on our rumps, and the shirts on our backs are quite likely wrung from the exploitation of the powerless somewhere in the world. As we grow up and, hopefully, attain a modicum of consciousness and moral sensibility, we know we are accountable before history and before our fellow creatures. We also begin to realize that many of our choices will not be between clear goods and obvious evils but in gradations of gray.

Additionally, we know that there is enormous moral evil going on all around us. We participate, passively in most cases, in discriminations of all kinds, and turn our televisions to other channels when the grim reality of the world begins to seep into our comfortable living rooms. We expect others to take care of this creeping sepsis for us; yet we elect representatives who are narcissistically driven by self-interest and corporate quarterly reports and who help us avoid the monstrous in our midst: the hungry in a land of plenty, the exploited in a democracy, the millions living on the fringe of survival. Our technology assists in numbing and distracting. The Roman *panum et circum* is far surpassed by our easy access to junk food and a variety of electronic entertainments running twenty-four hours a day with infinite capacity to seduce, to distract, and to deaden. To be even mildly aware of what is described here is to experience contextual guilt; to perpetuate this is to live in *mauvaise foi*.

Guilt as Anxiety Management System

Much more often, the state we label "guilt" is not the two forms of guilt identified above—the courageous acknowledgment of harm brought to others or our shadowy collusion with exploitation and values contrary to our professed intent. This sort of guilt, as we noted earlier, always manifests somatically, as queasiness in the stomach, a tremor of the limbs, even light-headedness. One of the signs of an activated complex is that it always manifests somatically, and while we may focus on that physical reaction and the energy coursing through us at that moment, we ignore the fact that the roots of this experience reach deeply into our psychological history and activate archaic fields of anxiety.

This activated state is often called guilt, but in fact it is an epiphenomenal reaction to a primary phenomenon, a secondary alert system to a primary sounding of anxiety's klaxon. We hear people say that they feel guilty when they say no to someone, or when they are angry, or when they fall short of parental ideals, and so on. Remember that our elementary sense of self, our internalized program of self and other, and our protective systems are all derived from disempowered times and places, messages overgeneralized, overinternalized, and subsequently reinforced by endless replication. As children, in necessary service to our narcissistic self-interest, we quickly run into the limits of our capacities, the sundry powers of the world around us, and its devastating proclivity to punish or withhold approval and affection.

For many, what was once spontaneous and natural expression becomes perilous, and we slowly grow alien to our original selves. One client spoke of how he used to sing loudly and joyously from the porch of his home until one day his mother screamed at him to shut up, and he did, thinking at that moment: "I will never sing again!" It was a silly moment and a rash conclusion, but in high school years later in a chorus alternating with gym class he was called on to sing so that the instructor could determine the right section for him. He shook with fear, opened his mouth, and nothing came out. His classmates laughed at his distress, and the instructor took his gesture as defiance and subjected him to corporal punishment, which was generally still permitted in those times. To an outsider, this incident seems trivial in the context of a larger life history, but each of us, if we have moments of insight and honesty, know that there are places in our psyche where we simply freeze and are rendered mute or grow angry and attack those around us.

From such encounters with the power principle, inevitable in the socialization process of each of us, one begins to internalize restraints, governors of our spontaneous natural expressions. Over the years one may lose contact with the psyche as a self-guiding system and slowly disconnect from the reality of one's feeling life. Since feelings are natural spontaneous reports from the psyche—we do not choose feelings, they choose us—to repress or constrict them is to collude in our self-estrangement. What is called guilt, then, is often an expression of the autonomy of this self-protecting system that protects us from returning to the wastelands of punitive or abandoning threats. Thus, when a natural impulse toward expression rises, a hand metaphorically reaches out and arrests the movement as a mode of reflexive protection. The epiphenomenal feelings of distress are leakage from the elemental anxiety that has been roused. All of this circuitry is triggered in an instant, and the impulse to action, expression, or value is contained. The payoff is anxiety management; the price is self-estrangement. Feeling guilty for saying no is really a defense against the possibility that that other will be displeased and subject us to the threats of punishment or withdrawal. Looked at from the conscious remove of adulthood, such a linkage is at best an overgeneralization and, at worst, a permanent state of paranoid fearfulness. But let us not downgrade the power of these archaic feelings, and defenses against archaic feelings, that allowed us to get to this new moment and then to suffer its contamination by the paradigms of earlier, disempowered times.

Given that most of us were conditioned to be nice rather than real, adaptive rather than assertive, this kind of guilt is a profound haunting of the present, an undermining by the perceptions and dynamics of the past. We need not debate the existence of ghosts when our daily lives and choices, and therefore patterns, are inhabited and driven by these spectral presences.

Guilt as a defense against the archaic agendas of angst reflects the necessary conditionality every child faces, and it shows up later as a tacit lack of permission to be oneself. The only way one can recover traction on the present is to ask the question directly: "Of what (or of whom) am I afraid in this moment?" Often the fear dissipates in the face of our adult powers, adult options, and adult resilience, but even then we often recognize how we have transferred an old paradigm of self and other to our partners, our organizations, and our society in general. How many children grew up hearing, "what will people think," and to what extent did that maxim contribute to their cowering before the world decades later? Usually when we smoke out those fears it comes down to the possibility that someone, somewhere might be unhappy with us.[4] Such a fact is devastating to a child and unpleasant to the adult, and we often fantasize outcomes that do not happen. But we have to imagine that if the worst came to pass, that someone would be unhappy with us, we can bear it, and bear it we must if we are to lay claim to adulthood and to a modicum of personal integrity.

When we remember that these reflexive but regressive powers were once necessary and protective in motive, we may find compassion for ourselves and others, but when we also reflect that those old protections lead to a diminished life, then we realize that such hauntings have to be confronted. There is nothing wrong with being fearful; that is human. But it is wrong to live a life governed by fear.

A child must do what a child must do. In the present world, to be a person of value rather than an emotional ethical chameleon requires us to make choices whether or not others approve. The angst that surges up from below when we do so can still spring forth with amazing, paralyzing power. But such guilt is inauthentic. Jung observed that neurosis is a life designed around avoiding authentic suffering. Neurosis is not about our neurology; it is about the split agenda within each of us. Authentic suffering means suffering the insurgency of the old angst and restraining the powers of regressive protection in service of speaking and living the truth as we experience it. We are all haunted by these spectral messages and attendant scripts, and when they prevail we are still stuck in childhood. Whenever we fight them, we move from a quisling guilt which betrays us from within to the necessary struggles of adults who wish to be persons of value and integrity. Once we have become truly conscious of this sort of haunting, the mechanism of guilt is no longer invisible and no longer acceptable.

Still, after all this we must remain guilty beings, and necessarily so. Without the pernicious gift of guilt, without ballast, we might easily drift untethered into clouds of narcissism and naiveté. Guilt can destroy, as we know, but it can also lead to a more differentiated consciousness. Jung put it this way: the guilty person "is chosen to become the vessel for the continuing incarnation, not the guiltless one who holds aloof from the world and who refuses to pay his tribute to life for in him the dark God would find no room."[5] The person without guilt is either profoundly immature in conscious development or has never really entered life, which occasions a guilt of a still deeper violation of incarnation.

Twenty years ago I wrote a book on all the troubling places the soul might visit in this long and unsteady journey we call our life. *Swamplands of the Soul* describes such marshy zones as depression, guilt, anxiety, loss, addiction, betrayal, and many other dreary visitations. After it was published one reader wrote to me and said, "Why did you not include *shame*?" "Huh," I thought, "why didn't I? It is so obvious." I thought a long time on that question and am still puzzling over it these many years later when I tell myself I really ought to know better. I finally concluded that, dismal as those other places were, I had a special resistance to writing about shame and managed to "forget" it in the list on my Hades Mystery Tour. But now I have to go there.

I grew up with shame, as many children do and as my parents did. My mother lost her father before she could remember him. Her dear mother was a seamstress, and she went to school in dresses sewn by her mother from flour sacks. She told me that she didn't know what the *I* stood for on her school records until much later when she learned that it meant "indigent." She drove me by the Jacksonville state psychiatric hospital where her father reportedly once was and told me to remember it because someday I would be visiting her there. (Ironically, she never went there, but my brother Alan served his MSW internship there many years later.) The family was on some sort of public assistance long before FDR and the beginning of Social Security, the safety net we have come to take for granted (unless, of course, one has been unemployed too long, and one's benefits run out). On many occasions my mother publically shamed me and discouraged my initiative in matters ranging from education to sports to socializing. One neighborhood child was deemed off limits because he was taking trombone lessons, and anyone privileged enough to have music lessons was in a class way above us, so I was to spare myself further shame by dissociating from him, despite the fact that he lived next door. (At the same time, his mother shamed him by forcibly giving him a permanent so that his hair would be curly like mine.)

My father, who wanted to be a physician, was pulled out of the eighth grade because of family economic distress; at age thirteen, he was sent to work for the rest of his life. His unrealized dreams were sources of great sorrow to him, but he never complained, ever, about the conditions of his life on the assembly line at a tractor factory. At one point, around age twelve, I memorized William Ernest Henley's poem "Invictus" because it touched something in me. I recited it aloud to my parents, and they both said I should forget it; life is not that way, it is better not to have expectations. It was still a culture shock when later I went to graduate school and mingled with folks there who had grown up with empowering messages of expectation. One of my deepest shames derives from a childhood moment in late August when my father and I were walking out of that factory with its 120 degree heat, the humid air filled with flying metal splinters, and I said, thoughtlessly, "I am glad September is nearly here so I can go back to school." "September never came for me," he said, without recrimination, only resignation. To this day I regret my insensitive reminder to him. I suppose this is my public apology to him.

In telling this story, I am in no way criticizing my parents. They were honest, hardworking, decent folk who meant well, but they could not help but share the *Weltsicht* that governed their lives. These days I honor both of them and am glad that they were my

77

parents. Most of all, I grieve the lack of opportunities life seemed to afford them and provided me. I write of them only now, when they and all their contemporaries are dead, so that they not be shamed further. In the face of such powerful parental exempla—some overt, some phenomenologically internalized from the atmosphere—one either serves the message or runs from it. I did both. As it is, most of us feel fraudulent or illegitimate and either wind up serving that message in avoidant or self-sabotaging choices or in overcompensated grandiosity or power complexes.

In the first half of life, so many of my choices were shame-based and self-denigrating. Education, which seemed the only ticket out of this impoverished worldview, proved to be something upon which I relied too much, thus cutting off both the vital feeling function and the shameful broth in which it was drowning. This inner discord finally reached its crescendo in a midlife depression and meltdown. It also led to my first hour of analysis. My first therapy sessions were with a well-meaning psychiatrist who knew only to medicate but, to his everlasting credit, after a few sessions he said to me, "The kind of questions you are interested in I can't address. You ought to go see a Jungian." "Of course," I thought, for I had had a strong, mostly academic, interest in Jung for many years. Little did I know that this was the beginning of the second half of life, and the beginning of phase two of an heretofore unconscious wrestling match with shame.

I have found that in most people's lives shame plays a role. It differs from guilt in important ways. Guilt is, as we saw above, a confession of something one has done or failed to do. Shame is the belief that who one *is* is wrong, who one is is profoundly flawed. Shame comes from two major sources, the first being the belief that we have to meet some criteria, measure up, serve some demanding program, even be perfect. Much shaming comes from religious institutions that emphasize correct behavior over grace and forgiveness, and like many other therapists, I have often had to work to undo this mischief in clients. Other shame comes from the internalization of "assignments," both spoken and unspoken, from parents or others. I cringe every time I see a stage mother or Little League father, for I suspect they are driving any enjoyment of those activities from their children. Either those children will sacrifice their lives to meet their parents' expectations, that is, live the unlived lives of the parents, or they will bail out along the way, feeling shamed as "failures." So many adults, many of them highly accomplished in the outer world, suffer from a lack of permission to really be themselves, to feel what they really feel, desire what they really desire, and strive for the life that really wishes to be expressed through them. Finding the seeds of permission and self-acceptance under such a pile of manure is always very difficult.

I observed to a friend one day, "You do not believe in hell, but you know you are going there." He nodded, grudgingly. He was already in hell because he knew at that hour that he really had to change his life, and no matter what he did, the price would be heavy. Driven as he was by both shame and guilt, and rejecting the metaphysical notion of hell, he knew he was going there because he was already there, stewing in the broth others had prepared for him so many years before. Although a very smart man, given that every child is dependent upon his immediate caregivers and the contingent messages of his environment, he remained a prisoner of their collective assumptions, as all of us do to varying degrees. While he thoughtfully and rationally rejected their premises when he made them conscious, he was nonetheless manacled by history, scourged by condemning ghosts, and consigned to the hell of a contaminated journey. No matter how he sought moral perfection and the higher ground of integrity and judicious choices, my friend who rejected hell felt its imaginary fires licking his feet.

It is not easy for any of us to escape the confines of history, nor ever be more than recovering children. As one sixty-five-year-old lady said to me in our first session, "When I use the word *self*, I shudder because the nuns used to strike us whenever we did, because it was selfishness." Apart from the question of how best to raise a child who is not afraid of being himself or herself, one must grieve this fine lady's inner division. For her, too, guilt and shame were the twin jail keepers of the cell in which she lived her whole life. Even coming to therapy was an occasion for guilt and shame, guilt that she was questioning those received authorities and shame for being such an apparently inadequate person. How her caregivers could have believed that these shaming messages could have served her soul remains beyond me still.

In the face of compelling guilt and belittling shame, what chance does a person have to breathe free and stretch wings of possibility? No chance, unless he or she suffers through to knowledge, to understanding, and outgrows these constrictive templates. It is easy for anyone outside these individual frames of experience to see what another must do and how easily it seems done. But then, reader, ask yourself where you are blocked, stuck in your development, confounded by your desires and bound by your restrictions. You may be certain that the binding agent for you, as for all of us, will be anxiety. While the specific components of the anxiety will vary for each of us, you may also be certain that wherever guilt or shame are present, and they almost always are, the strength to take on what needs done is sapped by these pernicious presences. Anxiety binds us to a possible future, and guilt and shame bind us to a constrictive past. In neither case have we gained sufficient purchase on the possible present. So, then, how do we do that? This will be the subject of chapter 10.

Notes

1. Marcus Aurelius, *Meditations*, trans. Maxwell Staniforth (New York: Penguin Books, 1964), 43.

2. Guillaume Apollinaire, "Hunting Horns." Accessed at http:// poetry365.tumblr.com/post/1105868646/hunting-horns-cors-de-chasse-guillaume-apollinaire.

3. C. G. Jung, "Psychology and Religion" (1938), in *Psychology and Religion*, vol. 11, *The Collected Works of C. G. Jung* (Princeton, NJ: Princeton University Press, 1958), par. 140.

4. This is the obverse to H. L. Mencken's definition of a puritan as a person afraid that someone, somewhere, might be having a good time.

5. C. G. Jung, "Answer to Job" (1952), in *Psychology and Religion*, vol. 11, *The Collected Works of C. G. Jung* (Princeton, NJ: Princeton University Press, 1958), par. 746.

CHAPTER 7

Ghosts and Things That Go Bump in the Night

There is no reality except the one contained within us. That is why so many people live such an unreal life. They take the images outside of them for reality and never allow the world within to assert itself.

—HERMANN HESSE, *DEMIAN*

In an earlier book, *The Archetypal Imagination*, I wrote about my first visit to the home of the Virginia painter Nancy Witt. In the room where I stayed there was a portrait of a respectable couple whose attire suggested the beginning of the last century. At first I thought the couple was Mr. and Mrs. Freud, given his beard, countenance, and the apparent era of the subjects, but on closer examination, they proved to be someone else. Moreover, as I moved closer, I noticed that I could see through their bodies to the furniture that sat behind them. "Who are these people?" I asked. "My grandparents," Nancy replied. "Why did you paint them like ghosts or embodied spirits?" "Because they are always here. They were in my parents, and through them in me," she concluded. And so they are.

We carry the genetic code, the behavioral and cultural tendencies, and the archaic messages embodied in complexes of many generations in each of our gestures. While no one like us has ever existed before, or will again, we carry all the past generations with us, always. Sometimes we hear our father's voice or an expression from long ago coming out of our mouths. Sometimes we catch a passing glance at ourselves in a mirror and see a parent's face. In "The Photos," poet Diane Wakoski writes of looking in the rearview mirror of her car as she weaves in and out of Southern California traffic and "there as I am changing lanes on the freeway, necessarily glancing in the / rearview mirror, I see the face, / not even a ghost, but always with me, like a photo in a beloved's wallet." It is her mother's face that stares back at her, now irretrievably her own as well, and she concludes, "How I hate my destiny."[1] While fate has chosen her parents for her, the poet apparently concludes that she carries not only their legacy of influences, but that, flee as she might, they continue to create her anew, her fate now unfolding as destiny. The past continues to work its way into our present, and nowhere more powerfully or influentially than in our service to their explicit and implicit messages.

I have also written elsewhere of strange experiences when I visited Sweden, the homeland of my maternal grandparents. My grandfather, Gustav Lindgren, came to America in 1900 and, a decade later, died in a coal mining accident; his daughter, my mother, never knew her father. Sweden was never mentioned—neither my mother nor her mother knew Sweden from Switzerland, so there was no conscious Swedish influence upon me whatsoever. Many years later I was invited to speak in Stockholm, and while there I had experienced déjà vu repeatedly, a mysterious but compelling situation. On our first night in Sweden, our hosts took us to an outdoor restaurant, and when we all rose to respect the playing of the Swedish national anthem and the lowering of the blue and yellow flag at twilight, I felt a voice come through me that said, "I have come back for you!" Instantly, I understood that I had served an ancestral "assignment" and had returned to the homeland on behalf of those who had once left it in economic hardship and were never able to return. While I had no conscious thought of such a recondite assignment, the power of that voice was clear and ineluctable. It was the first of many strange experiences of having been there before, even though I had always considered such things with a large measure of skepticism. To this day I do not understand such experiences at all, but they were real to me, and they occasioned more respect for the presence of the past than I had had before. A central part of the American story, the story we tell ourselves, is that we all start anew, that America is a place for the reinvention of oneself and therefore of one's destiny. And while this story is profoundly true,

I am now convinced that we carry much more of that past with us than we could ever imagine. Nancy Witt was right to paint her ancestors as ghosts infiltrating the room, for surely such invisible assemblies are all present.

Many, now and in the past, believe in the literal existence of ghosts, and perhaps they are right. But I am not persuaded. It is clear that we can turn to depth psychology for a more reasonable explanation of how the past persists in the present. Jung took the question of these spectral presences very seriously. His mother was mediumistic and so was his cousin whom he studied in his medical dissertation while in medical school in Basel. He came to a set of compelling conclusions about these ghostly manifestations, embodied in the concept of dissociation. In an essay written in 1919, titled "The Psychological Foundations of Belief in Spirits," he observed that in all traditions there is "a universal belief in the existence of phantoms or ethereal beings who dwell in the neighbourhood of men and who exercise an invisible yet powerful influence upon them. These beings are generally supposed to be spirits or souls of the dead."² Our predecessors believed in, because they experienced, the presence of two worlds: the world of the senses and the invisible world haunted by what we now call complexes and projections. An example of this is found in how many people feel persecuted by their parents or others long after the persons are dead. Recall that the German word Jung used to describe these experiential states was *Ergriffenheit*, which may be translated as the ego being "seized or possessed" by the power of the invisible other. How often have exorcisms been undertaken to rid people ostensibly occupied by evil spirits?

We can be possessed not only by "spirits" but by contagious ideas, fads, fashions, and fears compelling enough to launch persecutions, pogroms, and mass enthusiasms. In fact the word *enthusiasm* was once derogatory, meaning that one was intoxicated by an alien, often heretical god (*theos*). As I write, a large number of teenage girls at one school are manifesting strange twitching behaviors, and no organic cause seems identifiable or probable. We could accuse them of being insecure and wanting attention, but the costs to them of this behavior have piled up in painful ways, suggesting their unconscious has connected with the unconscious of others and collectively they, like the maiden in Hans Christian Andersen's "The Red Shoes," cannot stop this unending twitching dance. Such phenomena have occurred throughout history, even sweeping up entire villages and sometimes entire nations, in a psychic Saint Vitus's dance, a mazurka of contagion. Group hysteria demonstrates the contagious character of psychic states and the power of an invisible form to occupy and possess consciousness and render it in service to infectious beliefs. These phenomena range variously from France's dancing plague in 1518 to today's popular fads and fashions, stock market panics, and political enthusiasms. As Nietzsche once observed, how intoxicating bad reasons and bad music can be when one is mobilizing against the identified enemy!

The human psyche is so vast, and the ego frame so small, that we can never know ourselves fully. Safe to say, insofar as we are human, we carry the full range of human possibilities, traits, tendencies, self-delusions, and wholly unknown continents within each of us. Much of this dissociated material constitutes what Jung called the *shadow*, those parts of our personality that are unknown to us, but which play out in the world surreptitiously, or those parts that when brought into consciousness are disappointing, contrary to our professed values, or stretch our self-concepts beyond the comfortable. Other shadow fragments of energy represent our unlived possibilities, often passing unknown and unlived by us into the collective sea of history.

Dissociation is one of the ways in which we protect the ego's fragility by reflexively moving the disturbing affect outside the range of the known; thus it operates all the more autonomously in our lives. (In addition to dissociation, we might also cite avoidance, denial, procrastination, projection onto others, and distraction as ego-protective mechanisms.) How many of our behaviors can be tracked back to serving our insecurities, parental imagoes, narcissism, or other unsettling agendas? We all have multiple personality disorders as these splinter selves contend, collude, and conspire to effect their fractal programs. Swedish poet Gunnar Ekelof expresses it so graphically in "Etudes":

> ... And we kings
> and barons of the thousand potential creatures within us

are citizens ourselves, imprisoned
in some larger creature, whose ego and nature
we understand a little . . . [3]

These vassals within a vassal state believe themselves free, but all
are subject to an invisible order. And we must remember that our
ego—that which we think we are at any moment—is but one vassal in a mob. Most days of our lives we do not set out to bring hurt
to ourselves or others, but sometimes when we survey the stupid,
harmful decisions we made and the unimagined consequences
which pile up like neglected harvests, we are then "seized by a
strange unrest" and we discover "that some of the possible creatures have gotten free."[4] These released vassals roam the world
and our private lives and form our history, both the history we
put on our resumes and that which piles up in the lives of our
children and our children's children.

In addition to dissociation, projections are another phenomenon common to all of us, every day. None of us are aware of a
projection when we are caught in its throes. But we live in service
to many of them each day. A projection occurs when activated
unconscious content leaves us and enters the world. When that
energy falls upon another person, institution, or situation, we begin to relate to that other through the valences and expectations
of our own unconscious content. The problem with the unconscious is that it is unconscious, and therefore we are frequently
in a delusional frame of reference to the other, and know it not.
When the otherness of the other begins to erode the projection, as
it will inevitably, we experience cognitive dissonance, disorientation, and dismay. Often our discomfort triggers the power complex, and we struggle to renew the expectation of the projection,
even by coercive acts toward the other. Only when the projection
collapses, and we experience the reality of the other can we even
begin to consider that we have played a substantive role in the
engagement. The rocky path of romantic love is especially fraught
with such projected dynamics, of course, and all of us have experienced the flush of expectation and the crash of disillusionment.
During those in-between moments, we are occupied states, docile
vassals in a dictatorial regime, and only rarely are we able to trace
the source of the compelling activity back to our own psyche. As

I pointed out in *The Eden Project: The Search for the Magical Other*, no projections onto the beloved are free of mother and father material, so in those ecstatic moments of romance we are always freighted with the ghostly presence of our predecessors whether we know it or not, and we are powerfully driven toward repetitions of, or flights from, or hidden desires to redeem that past. But we are never free of that past in any hour of that relationship, especially at its outset.

Certainly more sinister examples of projection are found in sexism, racism, and bigotry of all stripes. Underneath most fear-driven ideologies and movements is an elemental fear of the other which then gets projected onto individuals or groups who are minorities or who are vulnerable. The more turbulent the era, the more insecure the ego and the more such projections are compelling, for they help a person separate or dissociate his or her fears onto that other. Our history is riddled with witch trials, pogroms, and persecutions. The more insecure the ego, the less it can tolerate differences, bear ambivalences. Thus fundamentalisms and militant groups of all kinds are fed by streams of fear and a violent need to dissociate from the otherness that lies within each of us.

The mythopoetic imagination of the human animal phenomenologically endows these moments of possession with the spirits through fractal narratives: offended gods, hubristic heroes, and haunted descendents. Homer writes of the wrath of Achilles when his friend Patroclus is slain by Hector: "mad Ares possessed him." The persuasive power of that invisible world is such that some believe others can cast spells upon us, or we upon them. This peculiar phenomenon is possible because of dissociation, the ability of contents to be psychoactive outside the frames of volition and consciousness. As Jung describes it, "Spirits . . . viewed from the psychological angle, are unconscious autonomous complexes which appear as projections because they have no direct association with the ego."[5] Many of our ancestors describe this state of possession as a loss of soul. An Egyptian text from three millennia ago has as its title *The World-Weary Man in Search of His Ba* (soul). Shamanic healing traditions are based on the premise that some noxious spirit has stolen a piece of the soul and the shaman's task is to identify which spirit has so acted, appease it, and help restore the missing soul to the conscious life of the suffering patient. This is not unlike modern depth psychotherapy, which seeks to address what instinct, what energy, what agenda has been captivated by a dissociated complex and thereby enervates the person. Tracking that complex and taking it on more consciously can bring about a restoration of energy and a strengthening of intentionality.

Our less pictorial image for this dilemma is what we call neurosis, having nothing to do with neurology but a lot to do with the interactions of conscious and unconscious worlds. We may describe these events as not feeling like oneself or being in the grip of a pervasive mood, out of sorts, or even our own worst enemy. We gain little by simply replacing the language of possession by malignant spirits with these neutral remarks, and perhaps trying to medicate the troubling state away. Frankly, the animated metaphors of our ancestors are far richer than our present psychiatric categories, but at least we are less likely to attack our neighbor for what we must recognize is our own psychic state. All of this is testimony to the fact that in daily life we slip easily between worlds and are seldom conscious of how often we are serving both at the same time.

We have all experienced such states of possession by spirits, for who among us is not touched, for good or ill, by our zeitgeist of materialism, hedonism, and narcissism. We are either fighting that ghost, that spirit of our time, or serving it, but none of us is immune to its influence. All of us have experienced states of psychic possession by economic uncertainties, political conflicts, and tectonic shifts in the social order. These moments are variously uncanny, frightening, alienating, and humbling and occur wherever the dialogue with the unconscious is diminished or forgotten. Any of us, myself included, can be readily possessed, and only when we remember that the invisible world is not only real but is driving the visible world our ego thinks is real can we regain purchase on a conscious perspective. Such spirit-states *are* real, psychologically, but it matters how we understand them. To fail to understand them as psychic states, energies to which the ego is prey, is to be at their mercy, to be living unconsciously, to be in the grips of the same malignant powers for which our ancestors devised such elaborate rituals, exorcisms, and apotropaic gestures. We still knock on wood to summon the tutelary spirit of the tree to stand by us lest the gods think us hubristic, or say "bless you" to assuage the loss of soul in a sneeze.

The integrative or apotropaic rituals of our ancestors, or the concerted efforts of psychoanalysis, can sometimes make those spirits, that is, split-off energies, available to consciousness again. Conscious scapegoating, ritualized during Yom Kippur and Ash Wednesday, is the effort to confront the invisible powers of guilt and collusion directly and to own them as ours. When undertaken in the context of belief, there can be sincere reconciliation for the participant. After all, atonement is about restoring the state of being "at one" with the invisible powers. In those moments there is a feeling of reconciliation and well-being because we are not dissociated or separated from ourselves as before. We all know that divorce does not end marriages, psychologically, nor does death remove the influences of the departed, nor does time alone efface the psychodynamic presence of the past. As Jung notes, "when a person dies, the feelings and emotions that bound his relatives to him lose their application to reality and sink into the unconscious, where they activate a collective content that has a deleterious effect on consciousness."[6] When I observe that most people, even those with achievements and productive lives, lack unconditional "permission" to desire what they desire and to live the life they truly wish, what is at work there other than possession by parental or societal formations? How would we ever really grow up—which requires knowing what we truly want, rather than what the parental or societal complexes want—and then mobilize the courage and the constancy to live it into the world?

We may say there are no ghosts, that we have abolished them to the superstitious halls of history, but we still submit to these unconscious energy clusters as if they were gods, malignant spirits, or controlling scripts. We can never obtain purchase on our own lives until we recognize, in the words of Paul Hoover, that we live with many expensive ghosts in memory's unmade bed.[7] To pay conscious homage to the thread of multigenerational voices which run through us, to know that much of what we do on a daily basis is in service to a spectral past, is to light a candle in the darkness of being, which is what Jung concluded is our central task. Such a mindfulness tells us on a daily basis to reflect, to sort and sift, to ponder, to acquire the discipline of discernment. Thus, we are obliged to ask troubling but necessary questions. What is that energy in service to, really?—for we cannot trust our first, conditioned response. What ancestral presences are at work in our choices, our patterns, our relationships either as repetition, as flight from, or as an unconscious effort to solve? What ghostly presences inhabit the many rooms of our psychic mansions? What figural gestures find their tangible cerements through our conditioned behaviors?

As a psychological confession, rather than a metaphysical assertion, we would have to say that there *are* ghosts and that we walk amid them daily. A continuing reflection on such spectral presences not only is the requisite task for the conscious conduct of life, it may well provide a less-divided sensibility and a richer passage through these twin worlds we inhabit at all times. Polish poet Adam Zagajewski gives us a warning as he slips along the haunted streets of Krakow: "I walk the paths of Kazimierz and think of those who are missing. / I know that the eyes of the missing are like water and can't / be seen—you can only drown in them."[8] The past is not gone, it is not even past; and it is the task of this moment to discern how these worlds meet and infiltrate each other.

Notes

1. Diane Wakoski, *Emerald Ice: Selected Poems 1962–1987* (Jaffrey, NH: Black Sparrow Press, 1988).

2. C. G. Jung, "The Psychological Foundations of Belief in Spirits" (1948), in *The Structure and Dynamics of the Psyche*, vol. 8, *The Collected Works of C. G. Jung* (Princeton, NJ: Princeton University Press, 1960), par. 571.

3. Gunnar Ekelof, "Etudes," translated by Robert Bly. Accessed February 1, 2013, at http://edgarssecretgarden.com/deepin/ekelof.htm.

4. Ibid.

5. Jung, "The Psychological Foundations of Belief in Spirits," par. 585.
6. Ibid., par. 598.
7. Paul Hoover, "Theory of Margins," *Chicago Review*, vol. 47/48 (Winter 2001–Spring 2002), 205.
8. Adam Zagajewski, "Unwritten Elegy for Krakow's Jews," *Unseen Hand: Poems*, trans. Clare Cavanagh (New York: Farrar, Straus and Giroux, 2009), 73–74.

CHAPTER 8

Betrayal's Lingering Ghosts

As we recall, every time we are gripped by a significant complex, we are at least temporarily removed from this hour and relocated to an earlier time. The more profound the complex, the more archaic, the less capable we will be to do other than follow its original instructions to us: close down, deny, flee, comply, or a host of other complicit, adaptive behaviors. In collective circumstances, during socially distressed times—times of fear, ambiguity, disorientation—we may share complexes with our neighbors, losing hold of our individual perspective and feeling states and becoming caught up in complex-driven, self-protective responses we later come to regret. From such moments of folie à deux rise holocausts, racism, war fever, and other forms of collectivized emotion. Any time we ask of others, in retrospect, why they did not see what they were doing, we are likely forgetting the many times we have come to regret our own reflexive collusions, our participation in acts that hurt others or ourselves.

On the quite personal level, each of us will recall moments when we were owned by the past with its reductive messages. How many times have I seen people bemoaning a divorce twenty years later or a betrayal of their hopes. Of course those wounding moments hurt, and still do, but implicit in their perpetuation is our willing collusion with those experiences as defining moments. How often do we allow the wounds and disappointments of history to define us and enable that diminution to persist in its wounding ways? How often have we failed to seize hold of our own destinies and thereby allow the fates to dictate once again? How often has our failure to show up in our lives revealed immaturity on our part, a failure to grow up, a collusion in victimhood?

༰ ༱

Most of us have experienced betrayal in life, sometimes even generalizing that experience to feel that we have been betrayed by life itself. Hamlet complained that his time was out of joint and what cursed spite that ever he was born to set it right. Betrayal is always experienced as a loss. What we lose may be our assumptions; it may be our naïveté; it may be our insufficiently differentiated way of seeing the world which requires greater subtlety on our part. The real damage lies in how we may generalize from that loss, that betrayal, and extend it into paranoia and projective identification. I have treated, unsuccessfully, two men whose mothers abandoned them at critical moments in their lives and left them to the mercy of strangers. In both case, the men became hyperindependent and transferred to their wives both distrust and the expectation of betrayal. In both cases they followed their wives, tapped their phones, subjected them to accusations, and, predictably, drove them away, thus confirming the a priori context and set themselves up for betrayal. The complex's flawed "thought" is: "If my mother would leave me, no doubt so will you."

At the archaic level of our psychological functioning, we often transfer to the universe, the company, the welfare state, the marriage an expectation that it will be "the good parent" and will therefore not let us down. Thus, when grief falls upon us or disappointment overthrows our plans, we feel betrayed, picked on, singled out, rather than summoned to a more sophisticated appreciation of the radical autonomy of the universe and the radical contingency of all things mortal. Even Jesus, in his darkest hour, cried out to his Father, "Why hast thou forsaken me?" Robert Frost observed in his sardonic way, "Forgive, O Lord, my little jokes on Thee, and I'll forgive Thy great big joke on me."

When we recall that the psychological mechanism of jokes is to relieve otherwise unbearable tensions through the cathartic release of laughter, or at least a grim smile, then we observe a very creative human effort to come to terms with the experience of betrayal. As Horace Walpole did indeed opine, life is a tragedy to those who feel, but a comedy to those who think. That such a term as *betrayal* is even used is a confession of a presumption that one is dealing with a universe that operates on our terms, has our assumptions, and ought to prove as reasonable as we are about these matters. That such an expectation is nothing more than a projection onto brute nature is a bridge too far for us, so we think of it as betrayal. If we rather assume that there is nothing that is "supposed" to happen, then we will move more quickly to acceptance than to the reflexive thought of betrayal with its power to bind us to the past.

While self-preservation is profoundly human, we naturally construct apotropaic defenses against a universe which can so casually crush us. We project the child's legitimate but archaic need for the protective parent onto the universe and then are surprised when the universe does not comply with our agenda. As a matter of fact, the great anguish of Western Abrahamic theology, whether it be Islamic, Jewish, or Christian, rises from this contradiction between the projection of the good parent as omnipotent God onto the universe and the seeming lack of reciprocity we receive. One branch of theology defined as theodicy specifically addresses the gap between the expectation of a just, loving, involved, and powerful parental *imago Dei* and the realities of suffering and injustice which abound. I was once so driven to address this discrepancy that after college I attended theology school with the specific intent of pursuing this theme in every course I took. While I experienced many wonderful moments of learning there, which inform my life to this day, I also learned that all "solutions" to this problem of theodicy were only talk in the head and fell far short of the demands of the heart. As we all know, and as Pascal observed in the seventeenth century, the heart has reasons that reason knows not. By seeking a "reasonable" solution to this discrepancy, I was hoist on my own petard, namely, the assumption that the universe serves such a puny human tool as reason or is subject to our rules for this peculiar game in which we are enlisted.

Moreover, I was wholly unconscious at the time of the role of projection operating in each of us, through which the mysterious other is always construed as a simulacrum of ourselves. This anthropomorphism haunts our thinking and leads us to what anthropologists and depth psychologists call "magical thinking." Magical thinking arises from the ego's incapacity to discern the distinction between objective and subjective realities. Magical thinking concludes: "I am sick because I have been bad, not because I swim through viruses daily" or "I am afflicted because

I have disappointed or am inherently unworthy." And how often have we internalized the behavior of others as a provisional definition of who we are: "I am as I have been treated. I am my history." How many lives have been tainted by this kind of subjectivized construing of a quite autonomous universe? All, until we begin to figure things out for ourselves.

As the Italian analyst Aldo Carotenuto observed,

> We can only be deceived by those we trust. Yet we have to believe. A person who won't have faith and refuses to love for fear of betrayal will certainly be exempt from these torments, but who knows from how much else he or she will be exempt.[1]

As our needs, and therefore our expectations, are virtually infinite and the capacity of such personages as parents, lovers, partners, and others is finite, so disappointment will often seem like betrayal. In clinging to the fantasy of betrayal, we are haunted by the past; we cling to a misunderstanding by indicting ourselves, others, and the world rather than critique our fallacious presumptions.

Another way in which the haunting by the past can betray us is how all or any of us in any given moment will succumb to a proclivity for what Freud called the repetition compulsion, namely, the tendency to repeat our history, to relive even its most painful chapters. How many persons have you known who found and married what they ostensibly wished to flee? How many times have we backed into our past by making choices that produced a repetitive future? How difficult it is to remember Søren Kierkegaard's observation, made in nineteenth-century Copenhagen, that "life must be remembered backwards, but lived forward." Frankly, much of the time, we look forward and live it in service to the dictates of the past through repetition compulsion. Why do we do that? Again, in the face of a large message, we have a tendency to repeat it—to serve its fractal script, run from it, or try to fix it. In each case we are still vassals of an old imperious, vested order, the more so as it remains unconscious, for we are still in service to its dictating message rather than our own natural impulse and desire. To replicate this received setup, this gestalt, this message in the governance of our lives is to fall into the repetition compulsion. To run from it is to blunder into a reaction formation, whereby in seeking the opposite we are surreptitiously driven by the primal text. Or perhaps we try to solve the problem by numbing behaviors, avoiding any analogous situation or believing we are gifted in fixing it somehow. (This last reflexive response is often the unconscious plight of the therapist who suffers again his or her troubling past patient by patient by patient.) Thus, a person who has experienced a parent as an invasive presence will seek out and bond with a person who will do the same—perhaps in quite different ways, which seduces consciousness into thinking it is all behind one—or will flee intimacy, or will sail off into a life of distraction and superficiality. Whatever the pattern, each is haunted by the compelling pillars of the archaic imago, which has been absorbed and internalized as part of the shaky floorboards upon which our conscious lives stand and try to fashion a life.

As with guilt, any apprehension or expectation of, any protection against betrayal unwittingly binds a person to the past. The only antidote to this pathologizing haunting is, paradoxically, investing fully in a new relationship, new ventures, new risks. To do so opens one up to betrayal and disappointment once again, yet the failure to do so sustains one's victimhood. If we are not willing to risk all, again, then we are precluded from intimacy. This is not to endorse naiveté or blind obedience, but rather to say that "in for a penny, in for a pound," otherwise one colludes with the perseverating effects of the original wound. The paradox of the betrayal/trust dyad is that each is presupposed by the other, each needs the other to be real. Without trust, no depth; without depth, no true betrayal.

Of course it is difficult to forgive betrayal, but the refusal to do so ultimately binds one to the betrayer. To forgive is to recognize not only the flawed humanity of the other but our own as well, and in the end it is the only way to free the shackles of the past which bind us. When we see a person hanging on to bitterness, however egregious the betrayal, we see a person still married to the betrayer, still defined by that constrictive event, still corroded by the acid of animosity. Life is so very short, and how wasteful it is to continue to invest our most precious capital in the failed stocks of bankrupt enterprises. While a person would refuse to invest money in a failed company, he or she routinely invests something even more precious, the soul, in an archaic imago that defines and directs each party to a very old place.

Marianne was a father's daughter. Pampered and protected as she was by a doting parent, she looked for his simulacrum to replicate his protective presence. And sure enough, if one looks, one will find what one seeks. Her husband, Gerald, had learned to take care of the expectant other, and guess where he got that assignment? While Marianne chaffed at his "guidance" and he at her controlling "neediness," each was content enough for several years to play out this archaic script of devoted father and grateful but dutiful daughter. When a particularly bold woman came on to Gerald at work and he responded, he found himself drawn out of the gravitational pull of the old order. Although he was perhaps only serving a dominant female other once again, he believed he was now relieved of his old duty, and he announced both his in-dependence and his departure to Marianne. I have no knowledge of how Gerald fared, but I do know that Marianne felt utterly betrayed by this abrogation of their sacred contract. Even when the situation was addressed by her therapist, Marianne wholly missed the fact that her husband's betrayal was her wake-up call, her invitation to grow up. She remained girlish in her whining, petulant, and bitter moods. Gerald's betrayal became her defining imago: unforgivable and universal. She terminated her therapy, accusing her therapist of insufficient empathy, and reportedly spent her next years continuing to whine and complain that the world was not taking care of her. Naturally, she found fewer and fewer people willing to care for her, fewer and fewer willing to play a role in the parent-child fusion that had become her defin-ing relational paradigm. Paradoxically, Gerald had done her the biggest favor of all, not unlike the dream of the woman in chapter 5 whose father and husband died (p. 000). The difference is one chose to grow up and the other did not. The invitation to rise above the haunting was refused.

There is a form of betrayal that haunts all of us to some degree and rises out of what we might consider another form of magical thinking. This term has been popularized in recent years by writer Joan Didion who wrote of the death of her husband in *A Year of Magical Thinking*. She describes in great detail how she came to terms with his passing, her evolving adjustments to trauma and separation. Then one day she realized that she had kept his suits in the closet, and this innocuous fact forced her to realize that she was consciously not in denial, but was unconsciously expecting him to return.

We all have moments like this. Magical thinking, again, is the failure to differentiate interior reality from external reality. Both forms of reality have an autonomy disturbing to the ego, and through both we nevertheless have to pick our way. Perhaps our most common form of magical thinking is found in our assumption that we can make deals with life, deals that are binding on our part, and on the part of all the other persons and "divinities" we encounter. We can swear eternal allegiance to the other, and still betray them. We can, as in Frost's couplet, feel betrayed by the universe itself. How many deals does one strike with the universe, promising good behavior in return for good fortune, for benevolent treatment by the universe? As children, many of us recall adhering to the admonition, "Step on a crack, and you break your mother's back." Well who would wish to do that? As children, we tried to make it all the way to school, with so many cracks in the sidewalk, and how mortified we were if we missed one, and in what state of psychological readiness would we have been for learning that day? (Today, thanks to Freud, we would recognize the hidden wish such a forbidding statement might embody. But to a child's fragile ego such ambivalence is intolerable.)

The case of Terence is illustrative of this haunting on at least five different levels. He is a man who experienced betrayal directly in discovering that his wife was having an affair, and when it was brought to light, she chose to leave an otherwise settled family. This story is a common occurrence, repeated multiple times in multiple ways, and the one left behind frequently wishes for the magic of therapy to talk the departed partner into "good sense" and to restore the status quo ante.

Naturally, Terence was traumatized by this turn of events, and while he was willing to look at whatever part he may have played in the situation, he firmly believed that no provocative causes reached the level of this kind of radical sundering of his view of the world, his marriage, and his sense of self. At the first level of betrayal Terence experienced a profound dissonance in his assumptions, in his beliefs about the universe and how it ran. "If I act fairly, I will be treated fairly," he believed. He had not made this assumption consciously, but the events in his marriage brought this thought—this tacit contract with the powers that be—to the surface. The traumatic events raised a primal angst within him, the feeling that one could not count on the solidity of the earth upon which we walk, the floorboards of assumptions and good faith through which we operate in this world.

Second, Terence reexperienced the dilemma of our common ancestor Job. The book of Job borrows from a legend of the ancient Near East wherein a good man, a man of faith and good works, is brought into a radical confrontation with the autonomous powers of the universe. An unknown Hebrew poet wrestled with this conundrum nearly 3,000 years ago and is obliged to move away from a casual assumption of his time and place, namely, that if we do the right thing, the universe will do right by us. When a ton of misery falls on Job's head, his friends, who have also bought into this assumption, assume that he is either unconscious of his shortcomings, in denial, or duplicitous. The Party of the Second Part goes so far as to presume to summon God to testify on Job's behalf and to attest that His servant has been faithful in all ways. Finally, the Party of the First Part shows up and reveals to Job that he was not some unwitting miscreant, but that he hubristically presumed his actions could somehow contain, finesse, possibly even control the autonomy of the transcendent powers. To his credit, Job acknowledges his unconscious inflation, repents, and is blessed in return. He moves from being a pious, conventionally good boy to a man who has had a "religious" experience. (Beware of seeking religious experience; one might find oneself provided with an encounter comparable to Job's.) Terence struggled with what this Joblike *metanoia* asked of him, and how, without bitterness or cynicism, he had to revise his sense of being in this mysterious universe, a universe in which contracts do not exist, or at least do not exist in the form we would have them.

At a third and mostly unconscious level, Terence was suffering the trauma of primal separation once again. We all experience this radical severance from the other at birth. Our needs wholly met, untroubled by the disturbances of a clouded, conflicted consciousness, we are thrust violently into this world, incapable of survival without the contingent protection and nurturance of others. Fortunately, most of us get enough to survive until we can begin to draw upon our native resources, but those initial passages are wholly perilous and outside the range of our fragile powers. Every infant longs to return to that primal safety but cannot, and then seeks surrogates in the form of a thumb or a favored blanket and, inevitably, desperately begins to look for alternative, reassuring constancies in its life. (Another analysand spoke of the rituals she invented as a child to try to bring order to the disorder she perceived around her. If she moved in one way, she had to repeat it, desperately seeking symmetry, predictability, and order. It was only when she reached college and saw other, less troubled, students that she was able to slowly wean herself from this obsessive compulsive treatment plan.)

The etymology of the word *religion* is a confession of estrangement, separation, and longing for connection. Theologian Paul Tillich even defined sin as "separation from the Ground of Being." How many petitionary prayers are offered up in this fevered hope? How many rituals of flagellation, self-abuse, and ritualized self-abnegation have been placed on the altar of fearful solicitation of this mysterious, autonomous other? As a result of his experience of primal loss, this recapitulation of earlier losses, Terence began to question the religious values with which he had been raised, values that he had sought to honor in the best way he knew how. Yet, absent those reassurances regarding the recondite other, one feels even more betrayed, even more at the mercy of the unknown, and even more alone. If we cannot count on reciprocity with others, on what may we base our decisions, our sense of self, our ground of being?

We all tend to treat the vicissitudes of our lives and the anfractuosities of our unfolding natures as insurgencies, usurpers of our control and ego frames, and we stoutly resist growth and change, even though this is the natural order of all things. Consider how we are periodically pulled unwillingly into the next stage of our lives, just when we thought we had figured out the former, frequently exhausting the various anxiety management systems in place to contain the unknown. Pan, the little goat guy, seemingly innocuous, lives in the wild, and whenever we visit his domain, minus any map that might have worked outside his thicket, we experience anxiety, even panic. Think this is an exaggeration? Examine how most feel about aging, the progressive decline of the body, or an unexpected and unfavorable medical diagnosis. If the nature of nature is change, forever destroying the old and bringing the next, whether wished for or not, then our reflexive resistance is in proportion to the degree that we are invested in the fantasy of sovereignty over nature. Thus, to a fortified ego, secure in its delusion of security, the depredations of nature, of time and tides, seems a betrayal of sorts, a betrayal of a presumptive contract which in fact does not exist. Such a contract, the deals we all make with the universe, repeats the story of Job over and over in our separate biographies. This is what makes him our brother. Would that we might also come to accept his humbled wisdom in the end. If we do not, we will be led to the same ends in any case.

At the fourth level—the experience of a marital vow violated—Terence had much work to do, for there was much pain to metabolize. To his credit, he quickly acknowledged that he had surely played a role in the outcome, a role that grew as he gained more and more insight into himself. Because such work is humbling and asks much of us, we can see why a person might wish to remain stuck in the posture of blaming and victimhood. It takes strength, courage, and humility to acknowledge that every relationship is a shadow dance of mutual complicity, even though one party may carry more of the responsibility and is judged more blameworthy for enacting what is in fact going on for both of them already.

Terence remained somewhat traumatized by his wife's betrayal, but increasingly he came to realize that clues to their increasing distance had been evident years before, as is always the case, and both of them had betrayed their commitment by avoiding difficult discussions. Even more, he came to realize that however sincere the launching of the experiment called marriage, both had been bewitched by a certain state of mind, limited by a certain level of maturity, and bound to a certain portfolio of expectations. All of those presumptions proved frangible in the face of realities unconsciously coursing through each of them, and undeniable as they later burst into conscious enactments. At one point he even joked that the church allowed annulments when one or both parties were not in their right mind, and who, he wondered, ever is when they are in the flush of such psychological states. How many times have I heard from people, good people, "I knew I wasn't in love the day I got married," or "Very soon I knew it was wrong, but I stayed for [x number of] years because of [the kids, my parents, finances, or some other reason]." But it is always easier to blame the other than recognize at how many stages of the process we betrayed ourselves, sustained denial, and perpetuated what was already outlived.

At the fifth level, Terence came to acknowledge the infantile parts he carried within himself, parts we all carry. The core dependencies, the fear of change, the fear of growth, the fear of loneliness, the fear of the disapproval of others—all are enough to veto executing what we know to be true for us. Nowhere do these archaic agendas emerge more profoundly than in the field of intimate relationships, because these go most deeply into our histories, our vulnerabilities, our residual parental needs, and our fear of growing up.

In the context of one of the workshops I offer I include the question, Where do you need to grow up? No one has ever asked me what I meant by that term. Generally, participants start writing in their journals immediately, suggesting that we all know where we are not showing up in our lives, where we are not conducting a conscious, accountable, mature life. Accordingly, betrayal is something we have been doing for a very long time, so long that now it is a habit, a provisional existence, a mode of being. How could we stand to deconstruct this papier-mâché assemblage we present to the world and to ourselves? Betraying our own souls has been with us so long that we often forget we have a soul and that it is asking to be served even more urgently than our dependencies and our infantilities. Jung once noted that "the dread and resistance which every human being experiences when it comes to delving too deeply into himself is, at bottom, the fear of the journey to Hades."[2] Yet, we may also remember that we live down there anyway, and that Dante reserved the most desolate place in Hell, the place devoid of any warmth of human feeling, for the betrayers. So parts of each of us live there in any case, acknowledged or not. Terence took his loss seriously, his marriage seriously, his responsibility to himself and their children seriously, and therefore took this voyage through the Tartarean depths seriously and has emerged a much fuller man, and now even more worthy of relationship. He deserves relationship, for he has lived through betrayal, refused to be defined by its historic haunting, and can now approach the prospect of starting over with enthusiasm rather than paranoia, risk rather than repetition compulsion, and a larger range of choices than a sabotaging adherence to the messages of the past.

One of the ways we are betrayed by the past, driven by our haunting, is by not acknowledging how much we are owned by our wounding—not only betrayal but the myriad other internalized messages to which we cling. What was once experienced, internalized as a statement, overly generalized rather than being merely a singular, ad hoc event, remains unchallenged and thus plays an inordinate role in the governance of our lives. The "betrayal" of betrayal is found not in how it wounds, and wound it surely does, but in how we cling to it and divert the work it asks of us to grow beyond its defining boundaries. As Jung once observed, we don't solve our wounds, but we can outgrow them.[3] The flight from doing so is the real betrayal. What choice then does history, not having been addressed and worked through, have but to haunt us?

Notes

1. Aldo Carentenuto, *Eros and Pathos: Shades of Love and Suffering* (Toronto: Inner City Books, 1989), 79.

2. C. G. Jung, *Psychology and Alchemy*, vol. 12, *The Collected Works of C. G. Jung* (Princeton, NJ: Princeton University Press, 1953), par. 439.

3. C. G. Jung, "Commentary on 'The Secret of the Golden Flower'" (1957), in *Alchemical Studies*, vol. 13, *The Collected Works of C. G. Jung* (Princeton, NJ: Princeton University Press, 1967), par. 18.

CHAPTER 9

The Sailor Cannot See the North

The Haunted Soul of Modernism

In 1867 Walt Whitman watched a "noiseless, patient spider" at its fretful work, launching filament after filament, seeking to connect. He could not help but intuit a connection between the urgent agency of this lowly form of life and his own spiritually troubled state. "And you, O my Soul," he writes, likewise flinging forth its yearning into the vast vacancy "till the bridge you will need, be form'd—till the ductile anchor hold; / Till the gossamer thread you fling, catch somewhere, O my Soul."[1] With similar urgency and in a quite different mood, contemporary poet Alicia Ostriker, in a poem called "Fix," surveys the vacancy of modern Americana and dissects the general, nonspecific malaise of our time. As a can-do culture we would quickly "fix" it, she says, "if we knew what was broken."[2] In Whitman we see a person still able to use the word *soul* with a measure of comfort and expectation of conventional understanding. Ostriker does not use that word, but she knows full well it is a matter of soul. She concurs with the observation of playwright Christopher Fry, who decades before her proclaimed that "affairs are now soul size."[3]

Of all the haunting of which we have spoken, the most powerful, profound, and pathologizing is our culture's psychic haunting by the lost gods of old. The eroded tribal mythologies, which once helped people locate themselves in time and space, the tattered divine narratives that gave meaning, purpose, connection, the faded cosmic story have lent a tenuous edge to all our dialogues, despite what a culture of denial and distraction may protest. While many cling still to the faded narratives of their ancestors or in anxious fury vociferously reiterate their ontological and soteriological claims, the truth is most people perceive in their bones the vast vacancies in which they swim, and they therefore cling to distraction, drugging, and denial as much as possible.

As Matthew Arnold pointed out in "Dover Beach," the sea of meaning ebbs and flows throughout history.[4] Yeats, among others, observed that when the death of Pan, that is, the archaic goat-god linkage to guiding instincts, was reported some three thousand years ago it produced widespread panic throughout the Mediterranean. St. Augustine wrote *De Civitate Dei* to assuage the anxieties of the faithful in the fourth century C.E. as the Roman Empire, the central ordering structure of their time and place, collapsed before their frightened eyes. In *The Way to Rainy Mountain*, N. Scott Momaday described the collapse of his Kiowa ancestral locus when the last wild bison, the totemic link to the gods, was slain. Whenever centers of meaning or tribal myths collapse, there will be great fear and anxiety, dispersion of the faithful, and the rapid rise of snake-oil salesmen of all stripes and persuasions. Such is our time: whether they are hawking cars or salvation, all one has to do is turn on the cable channels to see them in coifed finery and full flummery.

With deliberate hyperbole, one might argue that the last time the Western world made collective sense to both king and commoner alike was around 1320. That was when Dante portrayed a comprehensive and comprehendible Weltbild, or world picture: a three-story universe, a fixed moral order, and a set of normative rules for choices and their attendant consequences. At that time, king and commoner alike could look in one direction and see a large structure that claimed both divine and secular sanction called the cathedral, and in the other direction find a similar claim vested in a castle. Together they provided the spiritual longitudes and latitudes that allowed people to know where they stood, spiritually and psychologically speaking. While I have tracked the reasons for the erosion of those absolutistic claims elsewhere, suffice it to say here that their present claims do not make many inroads into the secular mind and this-worldly values of our time.[5]

By 1600 we have both the first recognizably neurotic modern in the tortured anguish of Shakespeare's melancholy Dane and the first empirically grounded approach to mystery in the articulation of the scientific method by Francis Bacon. The Polish astronomer Copernicus shifted us from a privileged, anthropomorphic position at the center to an increasingly peripheral and ambiguous location in what are now counted as billions of galaxies. (That is billions, not dozens, hundreds, or even thousands.) There is no "up there" anymore, only here and somewhere else "not here."

By 1800 the sage of Königsberg, Immanuel Kant, ended the fantasies of traditional metaphysics, the delineation of reality, by asserting that we cannot experience reality directly but only our subjective rendering of it. In so doing, he made psychology, especially depth psychology and phenomenology, necessary. By the 1960s, the social fixities of class, race, gender, sexual identity and orientation, and absolute moral claims, as well as the presumptive probity of institutions, had been deconstructed, leading of course to widespread cultural ambiguity, attendant anxiety, regressive moves to rigidity, fundamentalisms of all stripes, and a culture of denial, addiction, and mindless distraction. (Except in the details, things are pretty much the way they were for Dante Alighieri when he awoke on those Tuscan mornings seven centuries ago.)

Jung described what happens when we experience a shaking of our beliefs, our orientation, and our sense of who we are in the world. What one sees so often is what he called "the regressive restoration of the persona," the rapid retreat to "the way things were," or once seemed to be, whether or not they have outlived their service to us. Faced with a spiritual vacuum, humans will seek to fill it as quickly as possible with political ideologies, as was regnant in Europe in the 1930s, leading to the catastrophic collision of fascism, capitalism, and communism shortly thereafter. In the Western world of our time, the emergent triumph of materialism beggars all other beliefs. The goal of life is not an afterlife but, apparently, to enjoy this one. But the materialist vision of our time leads to this dilemma: *if the numinous is not experienced in the outer world, it will manifest either as somatic illness, internalized pathology, or we will be owned by our search for it among the objects upon which we have projected our existential yearning in the outer world.* Thus, shiny new objects, seductive technologies, sex and romance, hedonism, self-absorption, and most of all, distraction constitute the chief "spiritualities" of our time. Our spiritualities will be found not in what we profess but in where our energies are most invested most hours of most days.

As a result, masses of humans, even the distracted ones, feel ill at ease, not at home in this world, and are looking, always looking for something, like the *chindi*, or "hungry ghosts" of which the Navajo speak. In his memoir, *Memories, Dreams, Reflections,* Jung put it this way:

> [Are we] related to something infinite or not? That is the telling question of [one's] life . . . If we understand and feel that here in this life we already have a link with the infinite, desires and attitudes change. In the final analysis, we count for something only because of the essential we embody, and if we do not embody that, life is wasted.[6]

Because most of us do not feel that we are part of a larger story or that we are living out some psychological and spiritual truth, we are generally adrift, dissatisfied, dissociated, and distressed.

When we consider that the role of tribal myth was to address four great mysteries, and hopefully connect people in feeling ways to them, we realize how sterile our time actually is. These four orders of mystery, which do not go away, are still being considered by our unconscious, and our felt disconnect from them is manifest in psychopathology, sociopathy, mass movements, fads and fashions, and collective projections onto numinous figures who are frequently flooded by that archetypal expectation, as so many fallen pop stars and destroyed celebrities exemplify.

These four questions that never go away are:

1. Why are we here, in service to what, and toward what end? (*the cosmological question*)

2. How are we as animal forms, empowered with spirit, to live in harmony with our natural environment? (*the ecological question*)

3. Who are my people, what is my duty to others, and what are the rights, duties, privileges, and expectations of my tribe? (*the sociological question*)

4. Who am I, how am I different from others, what is my life about, and how am I to find my way through the difficulties of life? (*the psychological question*)

These questions, seldom asked consciously, are nonetheless always being asked in our unconscious, and we often find the putative "answers"—get a job, make money, have a good time, resist aging and the natural decline toward death—to be profoundly unsatisfying, anti-natural, superficial, and soul-denying. But then who really believes he or she has a soul these days? In place of the gods of old, we rely instead on materialism, hedonism, narcissism, and distraction to get us through the night. And just how well has that worked for us?

Of all of the great pioneers of the psyche, only Jung really comprehended that the issue underlying most of our yearnings, and most of our pathologies, was a profound but frustrated search for meaning and the replicative symptomatology of psyche's stubborn refusal to be hoodwinked by the lesser goods our time proffers us. Jung argued that neurosis is inauthentic suffering, but note that he does not rule out suffering, only that which pursues phantasmal will-o'-the-wisps and the myriad superficial surrogates so readily available. We can be sure our psyche will know the difference, and let us know, if we bother to pay attention. This is why there are so many restless, unfulfilled people in the Western world despite material abundance unparalleled in history.

The vast majority of our contemporaries fall between the cracks of the medical paradigm and the old ecclesiastic doctrinal models. Just how satisfying or connective will a prescription or a platitude prove to us today? As the patient turns to either doctor or clergy,

> both . . . stand before him with empty hands . . . even when we see clearly why the patient is ill: when he sees that he has no love, only sexuality; no faith, because he is afraid to grope in the dark; no hope because he is disillusioned by the world and by life; and no understanding because he has failed to read the meaning of his own existence.[7]

How provocative that last phrase is: "because he has failed to read the meaning of his own existence." And from whence will that meaning come: external authoritarian sources, traditional formulae which do not address the shifting textures of a postmodern world, someone else's sincere opinion? How far we have been driven from our own resources, our own experiment with the wondrous and terrifying invitation to our own journey! In that vacuum, mass ideologies and personal anodynes naturally fill the gap quickly, for our species ill tolerates ambiguity or uncertainty. We have all forgotten what our presumptive saints, mystics, and prophetic voices earnestly proclaimed: that if we wait upon the dark, it grows luminous; if we abide the silence, it speaks. We look to others to fix it all for us, and they fail us, because we have asked too much of them, because they are broken themselves, and because we have ignored, even fled, our own resources. No wonder we find it so difficult to love others when we have seldom learned to love ourselves in a form which serves neither narcissism nor self-denigration.

Driven to my own desperate ends at midlife, I undertook my first hours of psychotherapy. I do not recommend such a choice to all, especially since many sincere practitioners in the field have not had their own therapeutic experience, but I do believe that finding the right person with whom to work would help *many* of us, at *any* stage of this journey, reflect more consciously, more profoundly, and more effectively on the nuanced layers of our lives. We will be obliged to consider the various hauntings that keep showing up in our lives and, therefore, the lives of those around us, such as our children, partners, and colleagues. What I have ignored, you as my friend, partner, client will be obliged to deal with sooner or later, and vice versa. Just how conscious, how loving, how fair, how considerate is that? How can I not work on myself when not only I but you and others suffer my many avoidances?

When I admit that the only person present at every moment, in every scene of the long-running soap opera I call my life is me, then I am obliged to admit that, despite the profound ministries of fate and the choices of others, I am somehow responsible for the patterns, the replicative consequences, and the many estrangements from self and others that keep showing up in my life. As the reader considers this dilemma and the summons to accountability in the words on this page, they not only make sense but may seem obvious. In practice, the implications are stunning, humbling, and intimidating. While I cannot directly speak of that of which I am unconscious, that which is unconscious continues to spill into the world and to affect you, me, and everyone around us.

How scary it might prove to conclude that I am essentially alone in this summons to personal consciousness, that I cannot continue to blame others for what has happened to me, that I am really out there on that tightrope over the abyss, making choices every day, and that I am truly, irrevocably responsible for my life. Then I would have to grow up, stand naked before this immense brutal universe, and step into the largeness of this journey, my journey.

What keeps us from taking this step into largeness, what make the largeness intimidating, is the peculiar haunting of history common to us all wherein we, once small, learned that the world is big and we are not, that the world is powerful and we are not. While these existential realities are explicitly true for every child and quickly ratified by the conditions and exigencies of life, it typically means that we progressively ignore that which is nonetheless large within us. What if it were proved that we have trustworthy guiding sources within each of us? What if it were demonstrated that the autonomy of the feeling function, the energy systems, the formation of dreams, the bodily states, the intuitions which approach us, are in fact resources with which each of us is equipped not only for the journey of life but for a more productive pattern of choices? If we had had some exposure to these ideas, some individuated modeling in our elders, some practice of disciplined respect for the inner dialogue, we would more easily know that our source of guidance is close at hand after all. Our history the various literatures of depth psychology, mythology, and scripture, and ancestral embodiments are abundant, but to step into their possibilities will ask so much more of us.

According to the reclusive poet of Amherst, Emily Dickinson, the sailor cannot see the north, but knows the needle can.[8] Why would she have written that sentence so many decades ago if she did not intuit in her bones the dilemma common to moderns? Can any of us find such a compass within and risk trusting our life to it? Can we afford to really ask questions such as, By what values am I *really* living my life? If I bring them and their consequences to consciousness, can I really endorse them, stand with them, and live or die on their behalf? While the false self is protective and adaptive, it also constricts, binds us to a less-empowered past, and alienates us from the gods. (This is why Jung said that a neurosis is an offended or neglected "god," that is, where we are aligned through our attitudes, practices, adaptations against our own nature's intent.) Can we really afford a serious discernment process, namely, the sustained, disciplined sorting through the many "voices" that claim our allegiance? The book of John (4:1) asks that we "test the spirits" and differentiate the archaic hauntings, learn the difference between adaptive protections and the summons of the soul.

Jung noted that every patient he treated knew at some level when he or she entered therapy what decision, what necessary action, lay before him or her. I have found this generally to be true. One thoughtful woman came to me and spoke of her work on her marriage, the worth of her partner and children, and her deep investment in family and social belonging. As she left, as her last sentence in her first hour, she said, "I want you to help me find the courage to leave my husband." As a total non sequitur to what we had discussed theretofore, her sentence made no sense; as a summons to accountability before the task that awaited her, it was her showing up, finally. One man I saw knew that his life had been protected by walking around the periphery of every emotional confrontation. As a child in a troubled family beset with mental illness, he survived by avoidance, silence, and codependence. Choosing a partner to repeat this pattern was, of course, wholly unconscious until his depression and self-medication brought him to therapy. What was both so obvious and so difficult to grasp was that his dilemma was not really about the marriage, as such, but about the haunting of history and its message of adaptation over authenticity. Raised to be a nice boy, he became a nice man, but such niceness ceased to be nice when the depression arrived. His decision was clear, yet the haunting of history was his enemy, not his troubled partner, and it took more than two years of steady work, repetition, and ego development to bring this otherwise gifted man to finally take care of himself for the first time in his life. In the face of his acculturation, he would no longer be allowed to have a statue placed in a nearby town square in honor of his saintly sacrifice, but he might be able to live a journey that was *his* for a change. He was at last discovering a secret which so many of us have to find the hard way, "that I stand in need of the alms of my own kindness, that I am the enemy who must be loved."[9]

The strange paradox of our adaptive lives is that what once provided protection is now constrictive and unwittingly constructs self-imposed prisons in which we live. Sounds simple enough to deconstruct, but in fact how much residual anxiety might be aroused if we stop the old protections? What would be the price to those who are comfortable enough with us the way we have been? And, as far as that goes, how might a person live any better than with the adaptations that seem to work up to the present?

All of us have a plethora of messages flowing through us at any time. It is busier inside our skulls than the air traffic control towers at ORD, or JFK, or LAX at rush hour. How can we distinguish our voice from the many others? The answer can be found only in a sincere discernment process over time. Any of us can respond to an impulse of the moment, an urgent projection onto a person, a new job, a geographic location, and then live to regret it. Any of us can serve a complex inherited from our family of origin, or a pressure to conform, or a self-serving motive. This kind of reflexive response is what runs our lives most of the time. Discernment. on the other hand, takes time, sorting and sifting, considering and weighing costs; however, in the end, action is always called for, possibly including action to ratify the present, but it must be a considered action. My analyst in Zürich many years ago said, "We Swiss would take years of planning to consider living in a foreign land, and then we probably wouldn't do it. You Americans are crazy. You get on a plane and arrive, and then figure out a way." I thought he was being critical of me, but he went on to declare that he admired that willingness to risk. We all know that there is a difference between an impulse and a considered risk, but the trick is to know that difference at the decisive moment.

It has been my therapeutic experience that most people, even those most accomplished outwardly, lack a core permission to live their lives: to feel what they feel, desire what they desire, and to pursue what their soul intends. Such permission cannot be granted by another; it must be seized by a person who decides that it is time to show up. Such a life must be put together by a person who understands that the mythic task has inexorably shifted from the tribal images and rites, the sacred institutions, to his or her shoulders. Even those who stay within traditional forms and collective expressions need to sort through the traffic and figure out what works for them, that is, what is confirmed by their experience and opens their life to greater personal development and to meaningful social engagement with others.

Of course, our most distant ancestors knew all this. They knew that if we wait upon the darkness with enough humility, faithfulness, and patience, it grows luminous. They knew that if we listen to the silence it speaks in time to us. Similarly, we all have a feeling function. While we can override our feelings repeatedly, sooner or later they break through our suppression or repression and show up in our dreams, our behaviors, our addictions, our bodies, or our children. Feelings are qualitative analyses regarding how things are going as seen by the psyche, not the ego. Sooner or later, they will express themselves in ways supportive or subversive to the ego decisions. We all have energy systems. If what we are doing is really right for us, the energy is available and supportive. If we continuously override what is right for us, that energy will first flag and then fail us. Our dreams will oppose us, support us, or compensate for the one-sidedness of consciousness, and in any case they provide an autonomous commentary from a place anterior to, and wiser than, ordinary ego consciousness.

Paradoxically, while many of our ancestors would claim that reports from their interior were expressing "the will of God," and perhaps sometimes they were, one would wish that so many who claimed to have acted on the will of that divine voice might have exercised a more discerning, patient consideration, a more disciplined testing of the spirits. Perhaps then we would have suffered fewer holy wars, fewer inquisitions, fewer oppressions of the life force within. So many have been slain, so many atrocities committed in the name of religion when personal accountability, discernment, and the testing of the spirits was short-circuited by complexes, narcissism, and the fear-based agendas of the faithful. One might say that, paradoxically, the true test of the faithful will be found, if it is to be found at all, in the ability, or lack thereof, to carry on a dialogue with their own complex-driven voices within.

What I fail to recognize within me will sooner or later meet me in the outer world through whatever projections I have upon the outer. To summarize once again, then: what I refuse to face within myself will meet me in the exterior world through you, not as you are, but as I have so construed you. Putting it even more directly, if guiding wisdom transcendent to ordinary ego consciousness is not experienced inwardly, it will manifest within us pathogenically as somatic illness or neurosis or outwardly as projection onto objects of desire, and we will come in time to be possessed by that which we wish to possess. So great is the power of the individual human soul that sooner or later it exercises a profound statement in all our lives. The only matter over which we have a measure of control is whether we can mobilize the courage to take it seriously, establish a dialogue with it, and live in accountability to the soul in this present world.

What Emily Dickinson's aphorism asks of us is not to find the necessary compass in others, for that is a flight from our personal accountability in the world, but rather that we find it within ourselves. It requires that we be more conscious of the provisional lives we actually live through our daily choices. Either we are in service to received instructions, archaic adaptive patterns, or we have accepted some responsibility to the inner life. Those of us who understand where we live in history know that we have personal accountability and freedom unsurpassed in human history. The project of modernism, from roughly 1800 through 1945, was first to critique and then to dismantle the received tribal authorities and transmitting institutions. For the most part, these days governments, religious institutions, and privileged persons no longer reign by divine fiat but by the consent (or the timidity or laziness) of the governed. We know that however pious or pretentious their claim, they are as riddled with shadow behaviors, agendas rooted in fear, and narcissistic motives as any of the rest of us. We all know, whether we accept the charge or not, that *we* alone are accountable for the election of our values and the venues through which we serve them, and that no self-proclaimed authority can trump our obligation to our own souls unless we permit it to do so.

The project of postmodernism, from 1945 to the present, as exemplified in Samuel Beckett's *Waiting for Godot* and Harold

Pinter's *The Dumb Waiter*, is to figure things out for ourselves, to sort through the traffic. While this great freedom, as Sartre observed, constitutes a terrible burden, we all know, or at least our psyches know, the difference between *mauvais foi* and *bonne foi*. And whatever psyche "knows" will show up as symptomatology, either in our private or our public lives, or as a supportive presence for the task of life.

Probably no one reading this book would deny that responsibility for the meaning of one's life rests entirely upon one's own shoulders. That we would likely all agree on this notion confirms our intuitive awareness of the erosion of such received authority as illumined the lives of our ancestors. In this we would join Whitman and Dickinson. So, each of us, then, is left to answer these really important, and very personal questions:

1. How do you find true north in the conduct of your journey?

2. Do you know that you have an inner compass and how to access it?

3. Have you learned to trust it and to converse with it?

4. Do you know that your compass goes with you wherever you travel?

5. How do you plan to consult it more often in the conduct of your life?

If we know we have such a compass within, must we not then take greater care to—in the words of Madison Avenue—"never leave home without it"?

Notes

1. Walt Whitman, *Leaves of Grass* (Philadelphia: David McKay, 1900). Accessed February 4, 2013, at http://www.bartleby.com/142/208.html.

2. Alicia Suskin Ostriker, *No Heaven* (Pittsburgh, PA: University of Pittsburgh Press, 2005). Accessed February 4, 2013, at http://writersalmanac.publicradio.org/index.php?date=2008/04/17.

3. Christopher Fry, *A Sleep of Prisoners: A Play* (London: Oxford University Press, 1952), epilogue.

4. Matthew Arnold, "Dover Beach." Accessed February 4, 2013, at http://www.poetryfoundation.org/poem/172844.

5. See James Hollis, *Tracking the Gods: The Place of Myth in Modern Life* (Toronto: Inner City Books, 1995).

6. C. G. Jung, *Memories, Dreams, Reflections*, ed. Aniela Jaffé (New York: Pantheon Books, 1961), 325.

7. C. G. Jung, "Psychotherapists or the Clergy" (1932), in *Psychology and Religion*, vol. 11, *The Collected Works of C. G. Jung* (Princeton, NJ: Princeton University Press, 1958), par. 499.

8. Emily Dickinson, *Emily Dickinson: Selected Letters*, ed. Thomas Herbert Johnson (Cambridge, MA: Harvard University Press, 1986), 175.

9. Jung, "Psychotherapists or the Clergy," par. 500.

CHAPTER 10

Dispelling Ghosts by "Going Through"

We can come to God
Dressed for dancing
Or
Be carried on a stretcher
To God's ward.

—HAFIZ

In earlier chapters we witnessed how so many of us, probably all of us, are bound to the directives, rapacious fears, anticipatory anxieties, and lack of permission dictated by our separate pasts. All of us, in short, live in haunted houses and at best coexist with those spectral presences. Only in rare moments of emergency, sudden insight, or the exigencies of necessary action do we tend to break through them. Once in a while we step naturally into an enlarging psychology naturally, effortlessly, as a consequence of our innate developmental process, but that is rare. We may outgrow a habit, move away from an old friendship, or even leave a stuck place, but most often we circle around the same old, same old over and over, and its powers are thereby reinforced.

So the question perplexes us: How do we exorcise the haunting of our separate histories? How do we see outside the lens ground for us by fate and by the internalized exigencies with their attendant messages of our history? How do we ever break out of those self-contaminating judgments that say "I am inadequate as I am; I am not enough in myself. I suffer worse than, or less than, all the others. It has always been this way and always will be. I am worthless, hopelessly limited."

All of us persist in the old magical thinking, the confusion of outer and inner, between what happens to us and who we are. So we feel contaminated by our wounds, our shortcomings, and our past failures, rarely acknowledging that our neighbors, whom we often assume have it all together, are likewise barely managing and hoping that the rest of us won't notice. If we were to hear their stories, as I have often been honored to hear, our defenses would melt and bless them and hope for them, perhaps even more than ourselves. *Compassion* and *sympathy* are words whose etymology suggests the capacity to feel the suffering of the other, but if we remain caught within the circling loop of our own self-pity and self-loathing, we will never feel their dilemma, nor realize that we share a common misconception. The old French proverb that to know all is to forgive all would challenge us to hear the story of the other in his or her faltering journey or, failing that, to at least understand that the other has such a story which would, upon our hearing, melt our icy hearts and fear-driven defenses. Like the conditioned mill horse, it is more familiar to continue in the same fruitless path, each dreary circuit deepening the trough in which we walk, but what a desolate track that is.

The difference between us and the mill horse is our capacity for imagination. The thing about all complexes, splinter personalities, and fractal assignments is that they have no imagination. They can only replay the old events, scripts, and moribund outcomes of their origin. But we do have an imagination, the power to image something new, or at least alternative. The German word for imagination (*Einbildungskraft*) describes the power of constructing an image, a picture other than, perhaps larger than, or at least alternative to, the embedded picture of self and world that each complex incarnates. The imaginative limits of the mill horse condemn it to repetition, but the human power to imagine another is the key to our liberation.

In his seminal work *Thus Spake Zarathustra*, Friedrich Nietzsche presents us with a peculiar parable of this liberating possibility:

> Man is a rope, tied between beast and overman—a rope over an abyss. A dangerous across, a dangerous on-the-way, a dangerous looking-back, a dangerous shuddering and stopping. What is great in man is that he is a bridge and not an end: what can be loved in man is that he is an *overture* and a *going under*.[1]

What a peculiar metaphor this is, and yet in it we finally see the possibilities of stepping out of the haunted house. The overman of which the haunted prophet of Basel spoke is the evolved person, the more conscious individual. But what a metaphor . . . a rope across an abyss? Yet recall that the problem is that the complex that comes up for us around any affect-laden issue can only keep us affixed to the past expectation and the past outcome. How scary it is to step out into the abyss. The German word for abyss (*Abgrund*) suggests the ground of certainty and predictability, dismal as it may be, falling away from beneath our feet. Yet without such an event, what would ever change, what would ever bring us to a truly different place? Like Orpheus or Lot's wife, we may look backward, nostalgically, to that dismal past and lose all thereby, or we may step into the unknown future, heart in hand, and experience what it might bring us.

Thus it would seem that we have to walk across ourselves, that is, our own imaginative possibilities to cross over to another possible place. The abyss is our engulfing angst, our diminished sense of possibilities, our foregone conclusions. The crossing over is the possible step into our larger selves. The dumb beast is our mill horse repetitions of the familiar; the overman is the evolved possible intended by the gods. This freedom of possibilities is terrifying because it asks of us a largeness unfamiliar to us and certainly alien to the constrictive purview of the complexes. As the poet Antonio Machado concluded:

> Mankind owns four things
> That are no good at sea—
> Rudder, anchor, oars,
> And the fear of going down.[2]

As natural as our fears may be—those futile but familiar instruments of management—they are utterly irrelevant to any great adventure on the high seas of the soul. While it is terrifying to be out there on that dancing wire between the known past and the unknown future, it is no time to look down, hasten back to the safe but dreary familiar, or freeze in petrified possibility. We are out there on the high wire of all of our possible futures, and we belong there. The gods want us there because they want something more of us than the comforts and certainties of our timorous egos. Pascal once noted of our ventures in his *Pensées* that it is not a matter of whether or not to set sail—we are already launched. Kierkegaard observed in his personal journals that merchant ships hug the familiar shores, but battleships open their orders on the high seas, out there where the powers really contend. And novelist Lindsay Clarke observes, "Believe me there are moments when loyalty to the inner light can feel like stepping into outer darkness."[3]

But what else is there to believe in if we have no relationship to an inner source of guidance? Many have trusted in the will of God, but when the god speaks can we tell it from a complex, or even something differentiated from our own will magnified? How do we "go through" when we are still confusing who we are, and whither we are intended, with what has happened to us? And how do we sort out the myriad voices to which we are subject at any given moment? How do we accept, finally, that we are not our history but our unfolding journey?

Let me provide some examples to see this process at work firsthand. Louise was the child of a narcissistic and domineering mother and a mostly passive father. Early on she got the clear message that she was powerless before that necessary other, and yet she was to maintain a smiling, cooperative composure at all times. Was it any wonder that she became a social worker and spent her adult life serving this dual assignment? How painful it was to recognize that her troubled husband had only replaced her mother, how painful to separate and start anew, and how awesome the weight of history that she always carried, and carried with a smile for all. All of this had transpired before she entered therapy. She had met another man, remarried, and found, to her dismay, that the old depression had returned. Uncharacteristically, she treated this second go at marriage with a passive-aggressive control that had never been part of her repertoire before. It was as if she could not help but settle into the archaic frame of relationship, to be powerless before the needful other. At least this time, ostensibly still powerless to step into her own larger role in an equal relationship, she would exert some measure of management of her life by passive-aggressive manipulation. She didn't like herself in this new guise, and rightly so, for her new stratagem was still based on the imago of powerlessness. Thus, she found herself back in the old swampland of depression, the pit of learned helplessness. Louise knew that this was her private hell. With Milton's Satan she could cry out, "Which way I fly is Hell; myself am Hell."⁴ Or with Christopher Marlowe's lamentation, "where we are is hell, / And where hell is must we ever be."⁵ But Louise was also clear that the one consistent presence in her whole lifetime was not her mother, not her father, not her two husbands, but she herself. This seemingly obvious recognition is quite radical for it is the first step in climbing out of hell. As Jung put it, we are "as much possessed by [our] pathological states as any witch or witch-hunter in the darkest Middle Ages . . . In those days they spoke of the Devil, today we call it a neurosis."⁶

As long as our personal devil remains unnamed, left to spin his devious web in the nether regions of the unconscious, we will do his bidding. But such a devil is within us as a haunting, an embodied phenomenological encounter with the forces of life, along with their attendant messages. Because Louise was determined not to be bound forever in this hellish repetition, she invited her partner to join her in therapy. First she confessed what she found despicable within her, her hidden power drives to compensate for her earlier sense of powerlessness in the intimate dance with another. Then she confessed her deep shame, and her deep longing for a trusting relationship with the other. Fortunately, her husband could respond with empathy and understanding, and together they painfully but progressively risked more and more openness, more and more vulnerability, and more and more trust in themselves and in each other. (Paradoxically, trust in themselves was the prerequisite for trust in each other, for they had to learn that they could actually access their own truth and then risk standing for it in the face of both outer and inner pressures to cave and comply.) They both learned that what had been protective for both of them in the past proved constrictive today and bound them to a disabling agenda.

As obvious as this situation, and its evolution, seem to us as outsiders, we each have our places of defended tenderness, our own complicity with a totalitarian, internal shadow government. Each of us has an internal Vidkun Quisling who, in the name of avoidance, or ambition, or expedience, will quickly trade our souls for security, after which we wind up with neither. Once that tradeoff has occurred a few times, it becomes easier and easier to collaborate. Until we reach midlife at least and have acquired some ego strength and some patterns upon which to reflect, we are not able to take on any of the ghosts that own us or bear the thought that while things have happened to us, we are most often the ones executing the orders of these inner dictators.

Let me give you another real life example from a man who would not consider himself heroic, and yet his struggle with the compelling powers of the past provide an example to all the rest of us. Charles is a fifty-five-year-old business man who grew up in a highly conflicted family. His respite during those troubled years came from sports and intellectual pursuits. At one time he was taken in by priests and was strongly inclined to become a priest, for the church seemed to offer a more inviting family as well as a potentially noble channel for his humanitarian concerns. But he soon felt as constricted by this new family as he had by the old, and he began to feel that their proselytizing had been more about their needs than addressing his. Nonetheless, the imprint of those years of spiritual formation, that is, indoctrination, was deeply embedded in his psyche. He dutifully married a good woman, and they had a large and flourishing family together while he pursued a quite different calling in the world outside the church. Still, the never forgotten call to the life of the spirit haunted him, and late in his fifties, Charles came to therapy. His discipline, his devotion to the process, produced a very energetic examination of his dreams and his relational patterns. He had spent much of his life, as we all do, either in service to the implicate, guiding messages or trying to run away from them. Like most of us, Charles was until now still seeking permission to answer the summons of his own soul.

Intuitively grasping that the primary task of the second half of life is the recovery of personal authority, Charles is now undertaking the process that was too large for him in his youth. Decades later, much more skeptical, but bearing still the imprint of the hopes and demands that once exercised so much power in his life, he returns to this decision in his life via a dream that takes him back to his old hometown.

I am back in Cincinnati preparing for a march. It is a march which is to take us several blocks past the headquarters of the Archdiocese. [I join the march and] find myself gliding past the headquarters but notice the headquarters are surrounded by a ghetto. A priest enters this ghetto to make a sick call on an elderly black woman.

When he reflected on this dream, Charles said the one thing he always admired and continues to respect about the church was its social mission, its social conscience. As a young man, he naturally was looking for both mentoring and external authority. Through the years he had slowly claimed his own authority and outgrown that need, but his commitment to social justice remained a constant.

In recent years, Charles went through major surgery at the Texas Medical Center in Houston, which not only saved his life but summoned him to a new fidelity to his individuation journey, a summons he was honoring by entering into the depth dialogue with himself in therapy. As a confirmation of this and of his slowly acquired authority, another dream has him entering into a spirited dialogue with surgeons who are considering his case. While most of them believe that his situation is not salvageable, he argues with them, taking his place among them as an equal. This is a far cry from the youth of deficient or uncertain authority. Who better would know what is best for our "treatment" than us, if we gain sufficient consciousness, own that perspective, stand by it, and claim personal authority?

In still another dream, Charles finds himself with his extended family by marriage and while he treasures these kin, he also chaffs at having to submerge his serious journey with the distractions that occupy so many of them. In this dream he is summoned to join them in a group game, and he tells them *they should not count on me to play.* Meanwhile he sees *a beautiful toddler playing as a butterfly alights on him.* The child plays with the butterfly in a different game and *the toddler is laughing and smiling.*

None of us are likely to be imaginative enough to conjure these scripts consciously, but nightly they do appear as visitants from regions outside the purview of ego consciousness. Note that each one of these dreams is calling Charles to a sustained differentiation between what has happened to him, his individual haunting, and who he is. The "family" dream does not represent his denial or rejection of his acquired family, which in fact he preferred over his family of origin, but rather his acknowledgment that his "game" was not the collectivized form, the family distractions and diversions, but something far more fundamental. The beautiful child is the part of him that he, and we, leave behind through our necessary adaptations. It is the immortal child, the archetype of being, futurity, and developmental possibilities inherent in all of us. The butterfly is one of the ancient symbols of the soul, an etymological source of the word *psyche*, and it visits the child in playful forms. The child's spontaneous engagement in the game, the play of the psyche, is what we all left behind but what screams out from the depths to be recovered. This is an essential part of Charles's second-half-of-life process of recovery of himself, a process to which we are all summoned. If we do not go there voluntarily, the pathologizing gods will drag us there sooner or later. Even then, we may flee such an invitation to homecoming as we have so often done before. Why we would flee this invitation is a mystery, but it surely derives from the child's perception of its powerlessness in the world and the imperative that it adapt to the outer authorities. In so doing, we lose contact with the original soul, the being that is meant to be nurtured and brought into this fallen world as our healing gift. How many of us ever come back voluntarily, as Charles has, to tackle this possibility? More often we are driven by crisis or suffering to undertake this reconsideration. Either way, the gods await our showing up.

Notice how these dreams, in addition to the ones excerpted and summarized in earlier chapters, call upon Charles to differentiate his journey both from his historic roots and influences and from his current extended family with its ethos and *nomos*, namely, the socially constructed roles that so often define our instructions and constrict our journeys. Notice how his dreams call upon him to claim what is of perduring value in his religious vision, the call to social justice, without submerging his personhood in all the other vested authorities and hierarchies that so often come with prescribed values and role expectations. Second, note how he is called to take a decisive role in the management of his health and well-being, even in the face of scientifically vested authorities.

After all, it is his body and his health at stake. And third, he is supported in affirming his familial commitments without sacrificing his quite separate journey. Families are healthiest when they serve as launching pads for each person en route to his or her separate journey; they are most pathogenic when this project is subverted by its most narcissistically needy members or by the collective timidity of others to grow up, show up, and strike off on their own separate journeys. Charles was loyal to all three of these outer forms of authority, but he had an appointment with his own journey, his own summons to address the meaning of his life, and, in his fifties, he was showing up.

In addition to gaining some permission for this reclamation project from his dreams, Charles also undertook the process Jung developed called active imagination. Active imagination is not meditation, self-hypnosis, guided imagery, or wish fulfillment, but rather an effort to activate the unconscious and to have a dialogue with it in an interactive, responsive way. Sometimes people write down the dialogue that ensues, others paint or dance, though any plastic form can receive the imprint of our inner dialogue and embody its dynamics. In one such active imagination, Charles experienced a shamanic visitation by a hawk who first seemed to attack him and then illuminate him. I cite here an abridged report of that encounter.

> The hawk is in the air, and I hear its screech. The hawk flies about me, then I can feel its talons on my scalp. It lets go and faces me. I look into its eyes. The hawk is ancient yet I seem to know who he is. The hawk speaks, "I am the spirits from the past, and I come to you because it is difficult for you to come to us." [When Charles resists the hawk digs its talons into his face and pecks at him.] I fall on my back and shout out to the hawk that I will follow his commands. The beat of the hawk's wings heal the wounds as if I was never attacked.
>
> I gaze into the hawk's eyes and see unhappy spirits walking among the trees in single file. They are roped together and walk in silence, gloom, despair. At the front of the line are my parents, and behind them are their parents, and parents going back in time.

The hawk tells me that I must loosen the rope that binds them together. I tell the hawk that I do not know how to do this, but the hawk bestows a feather on me and tells me that I "have one life in which to free these spirits. And do not forget that the spirits need you."

This spontaneous conversation generated by a dialogue with the unconscious lights on a traditional symbol of a far-seeing, prophetic creature, the hawk. The ego's ambivalence about undertaking such radical conversations is common to us all, but voluntarily or not, the gods will speak to us, especially the disowned and rejected ones. Reluctantly, Charles is compelled to engage with this creature and to pay attention. Through this archetypal lens, Charles is able to see the trail of ancestors, his spiritual and psychological antecedents, stretching out before his vision, all bound, like Rodin's Burghers of Calais, by tyrannical forces of history. Moreover, he is told that he has this one life to live, too short perhaps, but he is still both privileged and charged with the task of freeing these bound generations.

Here again we see the dual theme of freeing ourselves from the ghostly weight of history, its oppressive complexes and diminishing directives, and thereby freeing others around us in some small way as well. As a tool to assist this transformation, he is granted the gift of a metonymic feather, that is, an embodied image that intimates something far less tangible, albeit equally real. Feathers have often served spiritual perspectives, given their origin in the creatures of the air. In the Brothers Grimm tale "The Three Feathers," the central figure is given feathers to set alight on the air, where, guided by the pneuma, or movement of the spirit, he can find the right path, make the right decisions. To be in touch with this spiritual gift permits one to move through this tangible world with much greater discriminative powers. Charles, as a man of courage and accountability, is working on this project as I write. A personal authority too awesome for us to hold in youth is now both one's summons and a proper source of guidance.

When we look at Charles's process from a synoptic perspective we see that he left home, as we all do, in search of guidance and support from others and in need of the clarity of a map which might provide assistance in traversing uncertain terrains. Naturally, like us, he had to try some things, many things, to see if they worked—all part of that inevitable and necessary bumble we call the first half of life. He sought guidance not from his troubled parents, but from parental surrogates—professors, educational and religious institutions—and learned that they did not fit either. He moved on to the social roles of marriage, family, and business that awaited him, and quite successfully so. But now he is well launched into the next stage, his second adulthood, in which he questions what in fact he is really serving with his finite but precious life energies and what aspects of his outer life and commitments still serve his journey. Many who feel such deep discords within are confused by this summons to consciousness and switch jobs, partners, or ideologies as though rearranging the furniture in the room will make a new home.

To piece together the threads of this elaborate tapestry, Charles not only has to sort and sift myriad influences and messages but discern which ones are truly his, which ones are merely acquired, and which ones deserve to be jettisoned. To that end, he confesses that while he cognitively rejected certain religious institutional injunctions long ago, they still lay claim on parts of his psyche. With regard to work and family, he affirms and loves both still, and yet must continue the journey his soul seems to be demanding of him as an independent being inescapably charged with bringing his own unique personhood into this world. Thus, his recent dreams are revisiting this mélange of pasts and rendering their haunting messages more conscious. If he, and we, do not undertake an occasional survey of that vortex of messages, we may be sure they will continue to haunt us in symptomatic ways, as persistently as my strange encounter with General Grant in the netherworld of dreams.

Over and over I see really fine people who express a general malaise, a desire for something different. Their job is okay, their marriage is okay, their relationship to life itself is okay . . . but then again it is not. When one begins to push against this malaise one hears over and over: "But that is just the way I am." "I am too old to change now because . . . [I am too near retirement; we don't have the money; the kids would not understand]." And so on. All of these outer "facts" may be true, but psychological mischief is almost never about what it is about. Sooner or later the real issue will be found in that complex, that affect-laden idea, that acquired message which stands in the way of growth.

If we pull apart the blocking message, we see a learned helplessness, an idea deeply reinforced in our history, a reticulated admonishment with which we remain stuck, in stasis, with its attendant calculus of cost. As we know, life *is* always more powerful, more imposing, more intractable than any of us can consciously manage, and still we are asked to show up.

What is stopping these good people is not lack of desire, for desire is ever present within us—even in depressed times—as the engine of life. Rather, a metaphoric octopus hovers over the soul and threatens to engulf it; a boa constrictor of compelling histories squeezes the spirit. But what are these *animalia?* What gives them their powers? Their presence is a legacy of the disempowerment of childhood and the magnitude of the powers around us at that time. One may argue over what past matters have to do with the present stuckness, but where else would such blanket statements of stasis and defeat come from? Why would otherwise thoughtful and functional people be so blocked and self-sabotaging? To say that "I am stuck and can't get beyond this point" is to be in the grip of some circuitry that leads to the psychic basement. Down there, in lower plateaus of our histories, is the terror of abandonment, the loss of the approval and necessary support of the other. Down there is the terror of incursive forces that annihilate or at least wound grievously. Yet underneath this oppressive weight of the repetitive past which curbs and contains, desire, the elemental life force, courses still. Desire is the engine of life, even as disorders of desire mark all of us in singular ways. Beneath each disorder of desire there is nonetheless a profound urge to grow, to express, to serve life more fully. Into the realm of desire and its various disorders is precisely the place we have to go to redeem the life we are meant to be living, to serve life and render the ghosts less haunting.

∾ ∾

The early work of Sigmund Freud and his colleagues opened the world of desire for us as a legitimate region of investigation. He and such colleagues as Josef Breuer initially worked with what were then called "hysterics," namely, people who suffered significant physiological impairments which could not be addressed by the conventional medical model (today these are called "somatoform disorders"). They discovered that some of the cases of blindness, paralyzed limbs, or anaesthetized vocal cords were compromise formations that embodied the ambivalence of a legitimate desire but one forbidden to the person. How else could a "respectable" person acknowledge a violent response to an oppressor or sexual intent toward another, or endorse values inconsistent with his or her conscious conditioning? The collision of these vectors within produced an acceptable "compromise" in the guise of symptomatology. "I cannot murder if my arm is paralyzed . . ." and so on. Freud and his colleagues worked in Victorian times, which have been characterized as excessively repressed. Lady Gough, the Amy Vanderbilt of her era, seriously opined that the works of male and female authors should not be placed side by side on a shelf unless, as in the case of the Brownings, they were married. A woman in Paris saw to it that the snowmen and statues in the city were properly clothed. And language was full of general admonitions such as one should use the word *limb* rather than the scandalously erotic *leg*. (Lest we think this internal split between the natural orders of desire and the imposition of constrictive values has been left behind in our "permissive" age, we should remember that quite recently, an attorney general of the United States considered it imperative that a classical feminine statue of Justice be swathed in cloaking garb at the Department of Justice in Washington, DC.)

Granted that the anarchic desires of the infant, narcissistic and imperialistic, within each of us must be mediated by the legitimate demands of the social contract, those who are blocked in the natural development of their natural desires have no doubt had something terrible happen to their lives. The hauntings of fear, the hauntings of imposed oppression, block their fundamental life energy. Etymologically, the word *desire* derives from the Latin *desiderare*, "to long for," and from *de sidere*, "of the stars." Our disorders of desire arise from our losing contact with our guiding stars. If one is a mariner on the wine-dark sea and has lost contact with that star, one is perilously adrift and at the mercy of whatever sea changes or currents of the hour may impose themselves. As mariners on the high seas of our lives, we need the star of desire to know toward what to direct our energies, lest we fall into the whirlpools of the deep—depression, despair, desuetude. How did the worship of the goddess Venus come to be venery? And how did passion, whose root is *passio*, "suffering," become so domesticated that we find its expression in the shadowy corners of romantic novels, pornography, soap operas, and infantile titillation in advertisements?

How different the world would be if each parent could say to the child: "Who you are is terrific, all you are meant to be. And who you *are*, as you are, is loved by all of us. You have a source within, which is the *soul*, and it will express itself to you through what we call *desire*. Always respect the well-being of the other, but live your own journey, serve that desire, risk being that which wishes to enter the world through you, and you will always have our love, even if your path takes you away from us." Such persons would then have a powerful tool to enable them to change their lives when it was not working out for them. Such persons would be able to make difficult decisions, mindful always of the impact on others, but also determined to live the life intended by the gods who brought us here.

Surely we have all tried, and continue trying, to fine tune the operations of our lives, but suffering awaits no matter what choices we make. The suffering of authentic choices, however, at least gives a person a meaning, which the various flights from suffering we undertake deny. One form of suffering enlarges, one diminishes; one reveres the life which wishes to be expressed through us, and one colludes in its sabotage. The poet Rilke reminds us of our inheritance:

> . . . we do not live, as the flowers, for a single year.
> For through us an immortal sap rises through our limbs.[7]

In the world of psychiatry and psychotherapy, our old companion depression has been replaced by something more exotic, more chic: dysthymia. *Thymos* is the Greek word for strong feeling. So desire apparently is no longer being "pressed down." Rather, we lack "strong feelings." Actually, we are never absent of feelings for they are autonomous responses of the psyche to how things are going. The ego may be overrun by them, threatened by them, may blunt them, deny them, project them onto others, but feelings occur in every instant. If one has a historically reinforced guardian with a scimitar guarding the entrance to the palace of feeling, then one will be aligned against one's own source of direction, one's guiding star.

The good news is that the desires of psyche never really go away. The very presence of psychopathology, or symptoms, are expressions of the will of desire to be heard through whatever twists and torques it must undergo to reach the surface. Like a tendril seeking light, it will burrow through stone if need be, through repression and denial if necessary. Desire may even drive us to our knees from time to time until the beleaguered ego is finally forced to cry out, "What do you want from me?" Then the god Eros is once again invited to the celebration of life by incarnating through the individual.[8] Each of us then is the scene of a sustained civil war, a contention between the natural desires of the organism for self-expression and the repressive powers of adaptive history. Even the temporary triumph of the haunting of history will not prevent the fact that, in the end, we all will nonetheless be haunted by the unlived life, which is the subject of our last chapter. Meanwhile, as W. H. Auden wrote in his commemorative poem "In Memory of Sigmund Freud," "sad is Eros, builder of cities, / and weeping anarchic Aphrodite."[9] When we risk honoring these neglected "gods," serving desire consciously and respectfully, we are again in service to life.

During this therapeutic day, I spent eight hours talking with folks who are navigating various rapids and impediments in their lives. Two, a mother who lost an adult daughter and a therapist who recently lost her husband, described how it never goes away, the grieving, the hollow feeling in the midst of even good days, the memory which sucks the energy from almost any moment. (And I too know those moments well.) Yet each has chosen to "go through," to open their hearts to the world around them and to the great grief in which they swim. My well-meaning physician

offered me antidepressants when we lost a son. I took them home
and put them in the garbage. I needed to honor my son with the
reality of his loss. "Going through" means that we have to experience what we do not wish to experience, for to flee it is even worse.
Unprocessed grief becomes depression or sometimes something
even worse. Some of us know the depth of that terrible but irrefut-
able observation of Aeschylus in his play *Agamemnon*:

> Even in our sleep, pain which cannot forget
> falls drop by drop upon the heart
> until, in our own despair, against our will,
> comes wisdom through the awful grace of God.[10]

Still another analysand is wrestling with a devouring parent
who is his partner in his medical practice and a devouring partner
to whom he is married. Only in therapy did he realize that the
former preceded the latter, which is obvious to an outsider, but
he has recently discovered how a childhood with the narcissistic
parent, internalized as a constituent element of the intrapsychic
imago of self and other, led to the adult's choice of that particular
marriage partner as well. As outsiders we would have to expect
this forty-two-year-old man to walk away from both, but to do so
is to stir up the overwhelming anxiety which every child experiences if he seeks liberation from the other upon whom he is also
dependent. What this good man has to do is *go through* his fear
and start his life anew.

Talk is cheap, and we can all be free with insight, even advice,
from the outside, but perhaps each of us should have to ask where
we are similarly blocked in our forward movement. In various interactive writing workshops I have asked people to describe where
they are blocked in their development. As yet, as mentioned earlier on the question of stuckness, on four continents, from Mos-
cow to Vancouver, to Sao Paulo to Atlanta, no one has ever asked
what the question means. Instead, within seconds they begin describing the stuck place in their life. That we can identify such a
place so readily tells us that we know we are stuck, and in every
case we are stuck not because we lack knowledge, but because
getting unstuck stirs the archaic fears within each of us and shuts
the necessary change down. For the parents grieving, and for the

physician intimidated by the magnitude of the task, the only way to go is through.

For those of us who are or have been in the torments of hell because we are stuck, it is hard to imagine that the alternative would be somehow better. Perhaps no one suffered more acute torment than Oedipus who, despite his intentions, lived out a sour fate, slew his father, married his mother, and begat children with her. When he was brought to recognition of his complicity, this man, who was known for his wisdom, realized that he did not know that simplest of all things—who he was. He was so appalled that he blinded himself before the searing vision of complicity and asked to be slain. But as a more severe punishment he was sent into exile to fully bear the consequences of his choices. Tradition tells us that in his ninetieth year Sophocles returned to this story which so intrigued him and wrote its finale in which Oedipus, after years of humbling exile and genuine penance, came at last to the sacred grove at Colonus where he was reconciled to and blessed by the gods and granted an apotheosis.

I am reminded also of the elder Yeats, ailing and suffering so many heartaches and defeats in his life, who writes in his 1929 poem "A Dialogue of Self and Soul," "We must laugh and we must sing, / We are blest by everything, / And everything we look upon is blest."[11] No young person would be allowed to get away with those lines. We would simply say to him or her, "Wait a few decades. We know you mean well, but wait and see what life has in store for you, and those whom you cherish, and we will talk about all this then." But Yeats had suffered through, as Oedipus did, and as many have. We can say that blessings may come to those who go through whatever miasmic swamplands the gods put in their way. They will have earned those blessings the hard way. No one who has sought some easy path around difficult times or has fled the task that always comes to us to grow or diminish can go through and receive the richness that follows. As youth, we are not yet capable of bearing such experiential richness and trials as *going through* requires, an abundance born of depth, transformation of vision, and a humbled respect for the mysteries of this universe.

The therapist in supervision who recently lost her beloved husband said that many of her patients are amazed, fearful, avoidant, and curious about how she could show up to do therapy with them when she is so recently traumatically stricken. Would they expect, perhaps prefer, a person who collapses and is unable to do what she is called here to do? Whom would it serve for her to stop being who she is, a grief-stricken but brave woman who cares for herself, her work, and her patients? By going through she embodies the profound message that we all have more strength than we imagine, that we all may be obliged to draw upon reserves of our humanity which we did not know we possessed. Not all of them will appreciate her powerful example of sitting with constancy and fidelity before them, but she herself embodies their greatest, most therapeutic gift: the message that we are here to be *here*, to go through it all, and to retain our dignity, purpose, and values as best we can. That is all we can do, and all that life can ever ask of us.

Nietzsche's odd paradox has it right. We have to walk out into that abyss of the unknown and find that something supports us even when nothing supports us. In continuing to undertake that risk there is more spiritual freedom, more amplitude of soul, than we could ever have imagined. But that is where we are meant to be, living not as fugitives, but as mariners on a tenebrous sea, going through to a richer place.

Notes

1. Friedrich Nietzsche, *The Portable Nietzsche*, ed. and trans. Walter Kaufman (New York: Penguin, 1977), 126–27.

2. Antonio Machado, *Times Alone: Selected Poems of Antonio Machado*, trans. Robert Bly (Middletown, CT: Wesleyan University Press, 1983), 113.

3. Lindsay Clarke, *Parzival and the Stone from Heaven* (London: Voyager, 2003), 136.

4. John Milton, *Paradise Lost*, line 75.

5. Christopher Marlowe, *The Tragical History of Dr. Faustus*, lines 121–22.

6. C. G. Jung, "The Meaning of Psychology for Modern Man" (1934), in *Civilization in Transition*, vol. 10, *The Collected Works of C. G. Jung* (Princeton, NJ: Princeton University Press, 1964), par. 309.

7. Rainer Maria Rilke, *Duino Elegies*; my translation.

8. Recall the dream of the graduate student in chapter 5 who was called to the dance of life, set in the mansion of early death, and the powerful complex that pulled him away from that invitation (p. 61).

9. W. H. Auden, "In Memory of Sigmund Freud." Accessed at http:// www.poets.org/viewmedia.php/prmMID/15543.

10. These words were cited by Senator Robert Kennedy to the troubled crowd in Indianapolis the night Martin Luther King Jr. was murdered, and shortly thereafter they were placed on Kennedy's own tombstone at Arlington Cemetery. Accessed at http://en.wikiquote.org/wiki/Aeschylus.

11. William Butler Yeats, *Selected Poems and Four Plays*, ed. M. L. Rosenthal (New York: Scribner, 1996), 125.

CHAPTER 11

The Haunting of the Unlived Life

The most painful state of being is remembering the future,
particularly the one you'll never have.

—SØREN KIERKEGAARD

Throughout these pages we have focused on how we are haunted by presences. But we are also haunted by absences. We are haunted by missing parents or parents who could not be present for whatever reason to meet the needs of their children. We are haunted by those deceased upon whom we once depended or need still for solace, conversation, insight, or simple encouragement. Last week I awoke knowing that I had dreamed of holding a lovely child in my arms and telling him how much I loved him. He responded warmly with a familiar smile. As I reflected consciously on the warm image which resonated into waking life, I recognized him from his tan and red childhood pajamas as my dead son. I had not seen or thought of those pajamas for decades. and I wept. A patient of mine tells me how every day she thinks of something she would like to share with her dad and cannot. The list goes on and includes all of us. As one woman said who had lost her daughter, "You don't get over it, ever; you just find new ways to go on living."

All we can say of this phenomenon is that absences are still presences and that death, divorce, or distance do not end relationships. One of my clients, a nun who lost her mother at birth, joined an order seeking a healing family and found other lost daughters instead. During a retreat she had a dialogue with the intrapsychic mother imago and experienced a living connection to this maternal source that had never been present to her in outer life. Even those estranged from parents or relatives grieve as they recognize that not everything gets fixed, that there are more loose ends than we will ever repair, and that we all bleed somewhere from the raggedy edges of life's unfinished business. All of these absences are presences and play a role in the governance of our lives, whether we know it or not.

In one of my workshops I have an exercise in which participants are asked to speculate on the particular values of their separate parents, what their mother valued, what their father valued, what preoccupied or worried them, and how they served the implicate "marching orders" of their lives. The purpose of this exercise is to help participants more fully recognize the ubiquity of the messages that haunt their lives and drive their behaviors. In many cases we can only speculate on what our parents actually felt or believed or the scripts they enacted. What is more important is what the child they once were internalized as the explicit or implicate message their parents were daily passing on. In many cases participants indicate that they do not know what the parent in fact believed or served, and many, of course, had lost a parent through death or divorce or emotional absence. Nonetheless, these lacunae are filled in by all of us—through implication, speculation, or necessity. In other words, what is not there is still there, and we are emotionally obliged to make do, jury rig a plausible fill-in for these messages, especially those who never knew their parents.

Strangely, perhaps synchronistically, in one two-month period I encountered three sixty-year-old daughters, one Swiss and two American, whose fathers had died during the waning days of World War II. Two of the daughters were therapists and the other had spent her life in a related helping profession. All three were deeply driven to know more about their fathers, a task rendered more possible today with the Internet. One of them tracked down survivors, attended reunions of her father's unit, and even took a tour with them to the battlefields of France, so deep was her longing. So we cannot say that absence does not also haunt us. James Tate wrote a terribly moving poem, "The Lost Pilot," in which he imagines his father's face still bobbing in the cockpit of the plane resting at the bottom of the Pacific Ocean. How haunted he is by this absent presence, as if he were "the residue of a stranger's life."[1] Are we not all, in fact, at least partially the residue of other people's lives: carrying their messages, living their unlived lives, serving their tribal values, suffering the limits of their ancestral complexes?

And then there are those absent who have been removed from the fuller expression of their lives by fate, fortuitous illness, bigotry, segregation, or discriminatory beliefs and practices. When my inner whiner shows up I often reflect that children my age were on those trains to the concentration camps, while I was safe, warm, and loved. What could I possibly have to complain about when I grew and flourished, and they perished with no chance to live their journeys? There are those who are blocked by social, economic, and collectivized practices which legislate against their possibilities, impair their permission, and stunt their souls. Just as there are personal complexes, so there are also social and cultural complexes that usurp our ego states and drive our behaviors. There is no religious, civil, educational, or social institution in our society which has not in some fashion constricted the rights, the opportunities, the encouragement to fulfill potential of some of its citizens. The discriminatory practices of gender, racial, sexual, ethnic, and cultural definitions have harmed us all. By limiting any of us, all of us are deprived of the richer possibilities, the dialectical magnification of our world by the delimitations of the few over the many or the privileged over the disadvantaged. None of us lives untouched by the ghosts of institutions past, most of them privileging some and oppressing others. Anyone who denies this, who believes himself or herself free of contamination by these oppressive histories, this slanted playing field, is, no matter their present beneficent intentions, the inheritor of their privileging consequences. People of conscience are haunted by this fact; others manage to sleep untroubled.

I am presently honored to live in what has become America's most ethnically diverse region.² Moreover, an overwhelming percentage of my fellow Houstonians believe that diversity is our greatest strength. Even so, the haunting legacy of poverty, racism, and ethnic discrimination remains with us and plays out in the air our children breathe. If that is true here, a city that celebrates diversity, how much more so in other cities around the world? In whatever urban or rural community, we all live side by side, breathe the same air, and cherish the same hopes for our children. And we all die sooner than we wish. Why then would any sane person persist in fear-based responses to others? Why then would any of us contribute to the absence or oppression of the other, which the prejudicial diminishment of any of us eventuates? Why do the fearful still exclude those of different persuasion from their community? The only answer is fear and immaturity, and we all have a long way to go before we are fully postmodern. To be postmodern is to understand not only the modernist critique of the old, still haunting, fixities that locked people into categories but to recognize that we now have to approach each other, see each other without the lenses of privilege or oppression, without categories, as simply other human beings who belong on this planet as much as we do. To afford ourselves that freedom we have to grant others the same freedom. But to do so, we all have to start growing up—a very daunting proposal indeed.

Another far more subtle haunting is the refusal we all, in some form or fashion, have made of the gift of life, of the invitation to show up.

When Jung formulated his concept of individuation he did not mean narcissistic self-indulgence—quite the contrary. Individuation is profoundly humbling. It obliges us to stand naked before the gift of life, the summons to personhood, and accede to the demand that we show up and contribute our small part to the big picture. From afar, that sounds reasonable, even doable, but in practice we all are intimidated by what it asks of us. Our well-being once depended on our fitting in, being adaptable, agreeable, accommodating. Individuation asks that we actually serve a separate summons to be different. The difference asked for here is not that of the adolescent who so painfully opposes parents and school authorities and adopts countercultural clichés, but rather that of risking who we are when someone else, perhaps almost everyone else, will not like who we are, feel challenged, even threatened by us, and oppose our very being. Who really wants to risk that?

Two literary examples of the profound ambivalence we have

to this risk of becoming come to mind. The first is a short story by Delmore Schwartz who fittingly borrows his title from W. B. Yeats: "In Dreams Begin Responsibilities."[3] A young man attends a film at a neighborhood theater. It is an old-fashioned romance. Slowly he begins to realize that he has seen these people before, yet not so . . . . As the film unwinds he watches the courtship of his parents, their youthful meeting, marriage, and the imminent issue: himself! Horrified by this prospect he rushes up the aisle shouting for someone to stop the film. In other words, he is fleeing the gift, and the burden, of his life which the parental conjunction brings. He awakens from his slumber on the dawn of his twenty-first birthday and concludes it is only a dream, a bad dream. The line from Yeats that Schwartz uses as his title reminds us that dreams come from the Self, the deep organic wisdom of the psyche that gifts us with the daunting summons to become. The youth, though chronologically an adult, would flee that gift, obliterate his birthright and his challenge, and in so doing flee his individuation.

Another example, with a different outcome, is found in the poem by Sharon Olds titled "I Go Back to May 1937." In her mind's eye she similarly sees her parents meeting, courting, and then their slow, inevitable trail toward the procreation of her. She too wishes to yell at them to stop, to tell them they are going to do things to each other and to their children to hurt them, things they will not intend to do. But unlike Schwartz's dream-youth who clearly wants to end the picture show and even prevent his own conception, she does not refuse the summons to her life but rather takes it on and proclaims: "Do what you are going to do, and I will tell about it."[4] Perhaps the horrific experience she describes in poem after poem diverted her from an otherwise "normal" course, or perhaps her calling as a poet of marriage gone bad, among other topics, is a result of this experience. In his famous elegy, "In Memory of W. B. Yeats," W. H. Auden wrote: "Mad Ireland hurt you into poetry."[5] Perhaps her parents hurt Olds into poetry, and her real calling was to be a country and western singer, a long-distance truck driver, a ballet dancer—who knows? But for sure, profound meaning and productivity is found in her being a poet, a scribe of the suffering she and her family experienced. Her individuation is forged through the sacrifice of her ego desires in the crucible of received life, and the music which comes from her then is wrested from the fiery pit of her familial Hades.

All of us fail in so many ways to show up, to step into the largeness of the soul. This shortfall is quite natural. The necessary adaptations to the conditions of life presented by fate, most often in the theater of family dynamics, obliges adaptation, and the natural instincts of the child are quickly found costly and soon forgotten. But these destiny-driven drives are not forgotten by the unconscious. The unconscious remembers everything. Think not? Then you have not really taken your dreams very seriously, for if you do, you will find the unknown architect of these spectral visitants remembers everything. The detritus of our lives shows up in remarkable ways, linking us to affects left behind, the people, the commitments, the hopes and oppressions consciousness has forgotten or conveniently shelved. But psyche remembers and, if neglected, will escalate into psychopathology. *Psychopathology*, literally translated from its Greek roots, means "the expression of the suffering of the soul." Why would the soul suffer if it did not have its own will, its own desires, its own plan—all of which are thwarted by the ministries of fate, by the derailments of our adaptations, and by our complex-driven choices.

The greatest haunting we all suffer is the lost relationship to the soul, to the original mode of being that proved too costly for us to sustain beyond age two or thereabouts. We evolve into apparent compatibility with the world around us, becoming chameleons as we take on the protective coloring of changing environments. Among the many who populate our intrapsychic life is a betrayer who expeditiously forgets principle in service to fitting in, being liked, modulating the pressures around us. As A. E. Housman put it, in his poem "The Laws of God, "I am a stranger and afraid / In a world I never made."[6] This adaptation, while protective and often necessary, is also a collusion in the abridgement of the soul's agenda.

We can get away with this collusion as long as we remain distracted, unduly anxious, or afraid of our calling. Becoming a person is actually a very difficult project, and yet it has a purpose transcendent to fitting in, to the ego's understandable desire to live as conflict-free as possible, even as that same ego admires historic figures who, summoned to the sacrifice of that same agenda of adaptation, chose differently and gained history's respect.

Jung is right, it seems to me, when he claims that the individuation task is synonymous with, or analogous to, what our ancestors called a divine vocation: answering the summons of God. It obliges us to serve that which pulls us deeper than is comfortable, wider than is convenient. From such push and pull comes a more capacious life, from such dialectic comes a longer, richer life story. "The achievement of personality," Jung writes, "is an act of high courage flung in face of life, the absolute affirmation of all that constitutes the individual, the most successful adaptation to the individual conditions of existence coupled with the greatest possible freedom for self-determination."[7] Notice that he distinguishes between the ego adaptations which bring us understandable relief and perhaps acceptance by the collective, and the adaptation that nature asks of us, which often obliges the sacrifice of the ego agenda for a larger purpose. As one of those exemplary figures who summon us to sacrifice the ego's petty agenda, Jesus, put it, "Not my will but Thine" (or Dante's phrase, in la sua voluntade e nostra pace, "in his will is our peace"). All of this is much more than the ego bargained for, desires, or feels comfortable in confronting. But the alternative, the flight from individuation, is worse. Then we are stuck with our frightened, diminished selves, in love with possessions which disappoint, power which fails us always, and presumption which always proves insufficient. To be stuck in such narrowed quarters is to bump up against our inauthentic being, over and over, which is a form of hell. As all the great tragic dramas exemplified, as long as we expect to understand the big picture and arrogate to ourselves powers reserved for the gods, we will be brought back to a troubled earth and a defeated agenda. When we observe and serve the mystery found in nature, in each other, in ourselves, in good work, we are living on the edge and grow inevitably, and we are thereby rewarded by the inherent richness of the journey.

Delmore Schwartz's dream-youth fled that summons, and one imagines that the dreamer, if he ignored the message, therefore led a fugitive life. Sharon Olds accepted her role as scribe and savant for her sinking family ship. While she could not save those on board, she could swim to the shore and convert her anger and grieving to song, thereby becoming much more than her early environment provided for her. What is it in any of us that allows us to persist, push through the obstacles toward something real, something authentic in our lives?

We cannot say for sure, nor can we find it in everyone's life, for there are, sadly, many, many defined, even destroyed, by their environmental fates. But what Jung called the Self, the natural wisdom, the organic drive, and the will to meaning, lives in all of us and waits for us to show up, keep the appointment. How many of us really keep the appointment in our lives? How many cancel out and offer a shabby excuse? I certainly have from time to time. And yet something within always aches and keeps knocking on my door, often at three or four in the morning when I cannot distract or repress. In those hours of desolation, one's meeting with the unlived selfhood is most poignant and most penetrating. With each day's dawning, the summons, the task awaits. It awaits me, it awaits the reader, as much as it awaited Marcus Aurelius on the Danube those centuries ago. He confronted his desire for relief and refuge, and cold, and no doubt fearful, he chose to show up. Will we?

In "Haunted Houses" Longfellow reminds us that, inevitably, "There are more guests at table than the hosts / invited."[8] In this study of haunting, notice how little attention was paid to the old perplexities of ghosts, evil spirits, and possessions which troubled the minds and spirits of our ancestors. They were right to notice strange and persistent events, occult invasions of daily life, right to try to understand the mystery of how certain energy systems could take over their lives from time to time. They were right to seek through their shamanic, exorcistic, and apotropaic rituals some means to rid themselves of these energies. Sadly, sometimes too often, they instead projected the source of these invisible presences onto their neighbors or the people on the other side of some boundary, and history's most tragic and unnecessary events have flowed from these misunderstandings. We now know that *we* are the carriers of those paradoxes. *We* are those accountable for the contents that spring from our unconscious and for what possesses us through our complexes and spectral presences.

We are all, still, possessed as easily as our ancestors by these errant energy systems. We are still as prone to blame others as our ancestors did or seek to medicate away our distresses and internal conflicts or anaesthetize them with distractions. Notice how many still indulge in bigotries in all forms or zone out through many brands of analgesics, or plug their souls into the Internet and keep a constant buzz going, or circle down to darksome layers of depression and desuetude—as if these unconscious treatment plans will spare them being haunted by their unlived life and held accountable for the avoided, shunned, diminished journey with which they were gifted. But we also have today a somewhat greater purchase on the idea that such energy presences are really within us and potentially accessible by our consciousness.[9] We are perhaps to a small degree more able to look within for we know there is something called the unconscious, and while it remains obdurate and opaque, it follows us everywhere, into every scene of our life. The practice of psychiatry soldiers on: describing, diagnosing, and medicating such "disorders," but cataloging them as phobias, addictions, dysthymia, or whatever does little more than sprinkle the magic dust of "naming" on invisible energies. It is as if naming them gives us power over them. This fantasy, this hubris, means that the spectral presences have even more power in our lives. The more we think we have them, the more they have us.

The real question is can we track those energies, those spectral presences? From whence do they come: the gods, the environment, the tribe, or oneself? What do they ask of us? How does consciousness appraise that demand, wrestle with its quandaries? What will we have to serve if we serve those hauntings? What change, what risk, is asked of us?

Do we really endorse those values, those outcomes, once we have made them conscious? What if we run from them? What is the price for that flight? What is the cost of a fugitive life? What tasks await us if we confront them, work through them? What new values may be asked of us if we are not to serve the diminishing message of the haunting?

Of all of the hauntings we experience, both as cultures and as individuals, the flight from these sorts of questions are the most telling, the most persistent. We now know too much not to know that we have to turn back toward these hauntings, face them, ask them what they want of us, negotiate as necessary with them, but retain the final freedoms of conscious beings in the end. Of all of these hauntings, the greatest is the one we alone produce: *the unlived life*. None of us will find the courage, or the will, or the capacity to completely fulfill the possibility invested in us by the gods. But we are also accountable for what we do not attempt. To what degree does our pusillanimity beget replicative haunting in our children, our families, our communities, our nations? To what degree does our flight from the honest struggle with our various and separate hauntings burden the world to come with additional hauntings? As Jung put it, what we deny inwardly will have a tendency then to come to us as outer "fate."

And what do we owe others during this process, this unfolding journey we call our lives? We owe them courtesy, respect, support, and most of all the example of a mature, independent journey we ourselves have undertaken. We can support their efforts, but we cannot live their lives for them, any more than they can live ours. We all have separate appointments with destiny, and we all have a separate accountability to the divinities.

It remains true that every day we awaken to find the old gremlins of fear and lethargy at the foot of our bed. They never seem to ever really go away. Fear says: "It is too big for you—this life, your life. Figure out a way to slip slide away. Avoid it any way you can, this life, your life, till it is done, finished." Lethargy says: "Chill out, turn on the TV or the net, have some chocolate, tomorrow's another day. In the meantime, you may slumber on." And no matter what we manage today, those darksome twins will be there again tomorrow and the day after. They are the enemies of life, and they are the primary progenitors of the hauntings we pass on to those who follow us.

Blaise Pascal, the seventeenth-century mathematician and mystic, once anguished that "the silence of these infinite spaces frightens me." So, he noted, the culture of his time invented distractions, diversions, scapegoats, and inebriations of all kinds. Similarly, at the end of the nineteenth century, while still an undergraduate at the University of Basel, Jung observed of his time what seems also to describe ours, a time in which the summons to encounter one's own mystery seems both intimidating and isolating. His citation of Nietzsche, himself once a professor at Basel, is familiar: "The world about us is full of ghostly doings. Every moment of our lives is trying to tell us something, but we do not care to listen to this spirit voice. When we are alone and still, we are afraid that something will be whispered in our ears, and so we hate the stillness and anaesthetize ourselves through sociability."[10] What, we now must enquire, might be whispered in our ears which is so troubling? What might be asked of us?

After all these years, resistant as I have been to writing this book, I am still called to account, still asked to show up. I am compelled by that profound psychological truth embodied in the words of the itinerant Jewish rabbi Jesus, that only when we die shall we live, only when the ego can surrender may we step through fear, rise from lethargy, into the next stage of our journey. I resonate to Jung's concept of individuation as a summons to both service and humility. I could not have borne such ego submission as a young person, but life's misadventures and nettlesome ministries have readied this bumbling pupil to a present availability. And how meaningful Beckett's admonition is to me today: "Ever tried. Ever failed. No matter. Try again. Fail again. Fail better." Rilke's paradoxical words also draw me onward still toward the unlived life that haunts all of us. Our task, he writes, is to be "continuously defeated by ever-larger things."[11] While the ego is apprehensive about the idea of defeat, the soul welcomes such ego defeat and the expansion that comes from ever-larger challenges. And Rilke adds, each of us may find "room for a second huge and timeless life."[12]

As encrusted, perhaps even as contaminated, as the concept of soul may be (in the Greek, psyche means "soul"), we might surely agree that whatever that word means that we might provisionally use it to refer to our essence, our deepest being, our deepest longing, and our deepest possibilities. We can deconstruct all concepts—even the idea of soul—and show how they are but partialities which privilege one limited form of viewing over another, but in the end, we have all to confront the ineluctable mystery of being itself, the unfathomable mystery of our own existence and the plethora of energies (a.k.a. the gods) which course through history and through us.

In the Zofinga Society lectures, the undergraduate Jung drew also upon the great philosophical presence of Immanuel Kant. "I confess that I am strongly inclined to assert the existence of immaterial natures in the world, and to class my own soul among these beings."[13] So each of us, in this most materialist of ages, has to ask: *Do I have a "soul"?* What could be meant by that? What does that mean to me? What does that ask of me? What does it mean to "show up"? Can I mobilize the wherewithal to engage that soul and serve it? What happens if I do not? While this paradoxical calling forth is challenging, it is what makes us most fully human, namely, when we also embrace and embody our spirit's intent. And how will any of us ever know that immanent mystery for ourselves if we do not step into the great opening life brings us? It is natural for us to experience this openness as a menacing abyss, but as Martin Heidegger reminded, the abyss is "the openness of Being."[14]

The paradox of being human is found in the fact that generally consciousness, processed through biological organs, can only apprehend the material forms of our being. If the soul were material, it would be an object and show up in our MRIs and CAT scans, but as an energic system, it courses through the material forms of blood, bone, and brain and expresses itself repeatedly in venues that are only in limited ways measurable. Yet, clearly we are forever driven by, and in service to, the immaterial energies of the psyche. This duality, this dilemma was articulated by Jung many decades ago. Given that we

regard the human soul as already, in this present life, linked with two worlds of which, it being joined in personal union with a body, it clearly perceives only the material; whereas on the other hand, as a member of the spirit world, it receives the pure influences of immaterial natures and distributes these influences in turn, so that as soon as the union with the body has ended, nothing remains but the communion in which it continually dwells with spiritual natures.[15]

Is it possible to conclude then that even among those of us highly skeptical of most religious formulae the invisible world coursing through our material form, what Yeats called "the foul rag and bone shop of the heart," is also our being, our identity, our journey?[16] If we can embrace the profound mystery of our own being, perhaps we will be less frightened by, less owned by, those other energies that impede our histories and haunt our journeys.

Hauntings are only integrated when we turn on the light of awareness and see the nothing that *is* there, the invisible that *is* present, allied with the challenge to take part in the construction of our story with a more differentiated consciousness. Hauntings may move us from fugitive pathology to summons when we stop running and turn and face our spectral visitants. Hauntings are transformed when we bring the unfolding mystery that we are to engage the mystery to which they invite us. As surrealist poet Paul Éluard observed, there *is* another world, and it is in this one. When we grasp his dictum, we know that here, in us, between you and me, is the meeting place of both the visible and the invisible worlds, the permutating movement of spirits that in the end are one. Both worlds wait upon our showing up, being present in this visible world while remaining mindful of the silent ministries of the invisible one as well.

Both our fate and our task, then, is to live more consciously, more thoughtfully in both worlds, knowing that our way of seeing is—along with the assimilation of enlarging experience and the generative powers of the human imagination—profoundly driven by the past. As the epitaph on the gravestone of Scott and Zelda Fitzgerald, drawing on the last sentence from *The Great Gatsby*, reminds us: "So we beat on, boats against the current, borne back ceaselessly into the past." And what is the task of consciousness then but a sorting through of messages, recriminations, impulses, and longings in service to the journey?

Who will ever tell the mystery of it all or name the ghosts which haunt us, drive us, impel us forward? Is not this life a series of repetitions, a set of variations, a series of investigations, experiments, and pummeling by the past? Bent forward, creatures of desire, driven by teleological urgencies, we seek our story amid the many stories that drive, surround, and overwhelm us. Much good work awaits us. It is our work, our lives, and we are responsible for it. Even then, as Thomas Wolfe, amid his own swarming "spectral presences," confessed in 1929 in *Look Homeward, Angel*:

> Which of us has known his brother? Which of us has looked into his father's heart? Which of us has not remained forever prison-pent? Which of us is not forever a stranger and alone? O waste of loss, in the hot mazes, lost, among bright stars on this most weary unbright cinder, lost! Remembering speechlessly we seek the great forgotten language, the lost lane-end into heaven, a stone, a leaf, an unfound door. Where? When? O lost, and by the wind grieved, ghost, come back again.[17]

Notes

1. James Tate, *The Lost Pilot*, accessed at http://www.poets.org/viewmedia.php/prmMID/15580 .

2 Jeannie Kever, "Houston region is now the most diverse in the U.S.," *Houston Chronicle*, March 5, 2012. Accessed on February 8, 2013, at http://www.chron.com/news/houston-texas/article/Houston-region-is-now-the-most-diverse-in-the-U-S-3384174.php.

3. Delmore Schwartz, *In Dreams Begin Responsibilities and Other Stories* (New York: New Directions, 1937).

4. Sharon Olds, accessed at http://www.poetryfoundation.org/poem/176442.

5. W. H. Auden, "In Memory of W. B. Yeats," accessed at http://www.poets.org/viewmedia.php/prmMID/15544.

6. A. E. Housman, "The Laws of God," accessed at http://ninaalvarez.net/2007/09/23/poem-of-the-day-from-last-poems/.

7. C. G. Jung, "The Development of Personality" (1934), in *The Development of Personality*, vol. 17, *The Collected Works of C. G. Jung* (Princeton, NJ: Princeton University Press, 1954), par. 289.

8. Henry Wadsworth Longfellow, "Haunted Houses." Accessed at http://www.poets.org/viewmedia.php/prmMID/19993.

9. A recent *New Yorker* cartoon (July 16, 2012) shows a mother putting her child to bed and presuming to comfort her by saying, "The only ghosts you need fear are the ghosts of your past—which will gnaw away at your soul, riddle you with self-doubt, and ultimately sap you of your will to live."

10. C. G. Jung, *The Zofinga Lectures* (Princeton, NJ: Princeton University Press, 1983), 73.

11. Rainer Maria Rilke, "The Man Watching"; my translation.

12. Rainer Maria Rilke, "In the Dark Hours of My Being"; my translation.

13. Jung, *The Zofinga Lectures*, 26.

14. Martin Heidegger, *Internet Encyclopedia of Philosophy*, accessed at http://www.iep.utm.edu/heidegge/.

15. Jung, *The Zofinga Lectures*, 26.

16. W. B. Yeats, "The Circus Animals' Desertion," in *Selected Poems and Four Plays*, ed. M. L. Rosenthal (New York: Scribner, 1996), 213.

17. Thomas Wolfe, *Look Homeward, Angel* (New York: Simon and Schuster, 1929).

Agee, James. *A Death in the Family.* New York: Penguin Classics, 2009.

Auden, W. H. *Another Time.* New York: Random House, 1940.

Aurelius, Marcus. *Meditations.* Translated by Maxwell Staniforth. New York: Penguin Books, 1964.

Burlingame, Michael. *The Inner World of Abraham Lincoln.* Champaign: University of Illinois Press, 1997.

Emily Dickinson, *Emily Dickinson: Selected Letters,* edited by Thomas Herbert Johnson. Cambridge, MA: Harvard University Press, 1986.

Dunn, Stephen. *Landscape at the End of the Century.* New York: W. W. Norton, 1992.

———. *Everything Else in the World.* New York: W. W. Norton, 2006.

Carotenuto, Aldo. *Eros and Pathos: Shades of Love and Suffering.* Toronto: Inner City Books, 1989.

Clarke, Lindsay. *Parzival and the Stone from Heaven.* London: Voyager, 2003.

Ekelof, Gunnar. "Etudes." Translated by Robert Bly. Accessed February 1, 2013, at http://edgarssecretgarden.com/deepin/ekelof.htm.

Ellmann, Richard, and Robert O'Clair, eds. *Modern Poems: An Introduction to Poetry.* New York: W. W. Norton, 1976.

Freud, Sigmund. *The Interpretation of Dreams.* New York: Basic Books, 2010.

Fry, Christopher. *A Sleep of Prisoners: A Play.* London: Oxford University Press, 1952.

Hollis, James. *Finding Meaning in the Second Half of Life: How to Finally, Really Grow Up.* New York: Gotham Books, 2006.

———. *The Archetypal Imagination.* College Station, TX: Texas A. and M. Press, 2002.

———. *The Eden Project: The Search for the Magical Other.* Toronto: Inner City Books, 1998.

————. *Swamplands of the Soul: New Life in Dismal Places*. Toronto: Inner City Books, 1996.

————. *Tracking the Gods: The Place of Myth in Modern Life*. Toronto: Inner City Books, 1995.

————. *What Matters Most: Living a More Considered Life*. New York: Gotham Books, 2009.

————. *Why Good People Do Bad Things: Understanding Our Darker Selves*. New York: Gotham Books, 2007.

Hoover, Paul. *Rehearsal in Black*. Applecross, Western Australia: Salt Publishing, 2001.

Hoover, Paul. "Theory of Margins." *Chicago Review*, vol. 47/48 (Winter 2001–Spring 2002), 205–208.

Hopkins, Gerard Manley. *Poems and Prose*. Selected and edited by W. H. Gardner. New York: Penguin Books, 1953.

Ibsen, Henrik. *Ghosts and Other Plays*. New York: Penguin, 1964.

Jung, Carl Gustav. *C. G. Jung Letters*, 2 vols. Ed. Gerhard Adler and Aniela Jaffé. Princeton: Princeton University Press, 1973.

Jung, Carl Gustav. "Answer to Job" (1952), in *Psychology and Religion*, vol. 11, *The Collected Works of C. G. Jung*. Princeton, NJ: Princeton University Press, 1958.

————. "Commentary on 'The Secret of the Golden Flower'" (1957), in *Alchemical Studies*, vol. 13, *The Collected Works of C. G. Jung*. Princeton, NJ: Princeton University Press, 1967.

————. "The Development of Personality" (1934), in *The Development of Personality*, vol. 17, *The Collected Works of C. G. Jung*. Princeton, NJ: Princeton University Press, 1954.

————. "The Meaning of Psychology for Modern Man" (1934), in *Civilization in Transition*, vol. 10, *The Collected Works of C. G. Jung*. Princeton, NJ: Princeton University Press, 1964.

————. *Memories, Dreams, Reflections*. Edited by Aniela Jaffé. New York: Pantheon Books, 1961.

————. "On the Psychology and Pathology of So-called Occult Phenomena" (1902), in *Psychiatric Studies*, vol. 1, *The Collected Works of C. G. Jung*. Princeton, NJ: Princeton University Press, 1957.

————. "The Psychological Foundations of Belief in Spirits" (1948), in *The Structure and Dynamics of the Psyche*, vol. 8, *The Collected Works of C. G. Jung*. Princeton, NJ: Princeton University Press, 1960.

————. *Psychology and Alchemy*, vol. 12, *The Collected Works of C. G. Jung*. Princeton, NJ: Princeton University Press, 1953.

————. "Psychology and Religion" (1938), in *Psychology and Religion*, vol. 11, *The Collected Works of C. G. Jung*. Princeton, NJ: Princeton University Press, 1958.

————. "Psychotherapists or the Clergy" (1932), in *Psychology and Religion*, vol. 11, *The Collected Works of C. G. Jung*. Princeton, NJ: Princeton University Press, 1958.

————. *The Zofinga Lectures*. Princeton, NJ: Princeton University Press, 1983.

Joyce, James. "The Dead," in *Dubliners*. New York: Dover Publications, 1991.

Kafka, Franz. *Letters to Milena*. Translated by Philip Boehm. New York: Schocken Books, 1990.

Kever, Jeannie. "Houston region is now the most diverse in the U.S.," *Houston Chronicle*, March 5, 2012. Accessed on February 8, 2013, at http://www.chron.com/news/houston-texas/article/Houston-region-is-now-the-most-diverse-in-the-U-S-3384174.php.

Ladinsky, Daniel. *I Heard God Laughing: Renderings of Hafiz*. Walnut Creek, CA: Sufism Reoriented, 2004.

Machado, Antonio. *Times Alone: Selected Poems of Antonio Machado*. Translated by Robert Bly. Middletown, CT: Wesleyan University Press, 1983.

Nietzsche, Friedrich. *The Portable Nietzsche*. Edited and translated by Walter Kaufman. New York: Penguin, 1977.

Olds, Sharon. *The Gold Cell*. New York: Knopf, 1987.

Ostriker, Alicia Suskin. *No Heaven*. Pittsburgh, PA: University of Pittsburgh Press, 2005.

Rilke, Rainer Maria. *Duino Elegies*. Accessed at http://www.poetry intranslation.com/PITBR/German/Rilke.htm#_Toc509812217.

Schwartz, Delmore. *In Dreams Begin Responsibilities and Other Stories*. New York: New Directions, 1937.

Schlink, Bernhard. *The Reader*. Translated by Carol Brown Janeway. New York: Vintage Books, 1998.

Tate, James. *The Lost Pilot*. New Haven, CT: Yale University Press, 1969.

Wakoski, Diane. *Emerald Ice: Selected Poems 1962–1987*. Jaffrey, NH: Black Sparrow Press, 1988.

Whitman, Walt. *Leaves of Grass*. Philadelphia: David McKay, 1900.

Wolfe, Thomas. *Look Homeward, Angel*. New York: Simon and Schuster, 1929.

Yeats, William Butler. *A Vision*. New York: MacMillan, 1938.

———. *Selected Poems and Four Plays*, edited by M. L. Rosenthal. New York: Scribner, 1996.

Zagajewski, Adam. *Unseen Hand: Poems*. Translated by Clare Cavanagh. New York: Farrar, Straus, and Giroux, 2009.

James Hollis, PhD, was born in Springfield, Illinois, and has degrees from Manchester University, Drew University, and the Jung Institute of Zürich, Switzerland. This is his fourteenth book, many of which have been translated into sixteen languages. He is a co-founder of the C. G. Jung Institute of Philadelphia and Saybrook University's Jungian Studies program, director emeritus of the Jung Center of Houston, vice president emeritus of the Philemon Foundation, and an adjunct professor at Saybrook University and Pacifica Graduate Institute. He resides in Houston, Texas, where he conducts an analytic practice. He lives with his wife Jill, who is an artist and therapist, and together they have three living children and eight grandchildren.

For a catalog of other Chiron titles, please visit:

www.chironpublications.com

For more information, please visit:

www.jameshollis.net

www.junghouston.org

www.ashevillejungcenter.org